A Guide
to Doing Business
on the
Arabian Peninsula

A Guide to Doing Business on the Arabian Peninsula

Quentin W. Fleming

amacom

A Division of American Management Associations

Library of Congress Cataloging in Publication Data

Fleming, Quentin W
  A guide to doing business on the Arabian peninsula.

  Bibliography: p.
  Includes index.
  1. Arabia—Commerce—Handbooks, manuals, etc.
2. Arabia—Economic conditions—Handbooks,
manuals, etc. I. Title.
HF3762.Z6F54   332.6'732253   80-69703
ISBN 0-8144-5666-9

© 1981 AMACOM
A division of American Management Associations, New
York.

First Printing

Acknowledgments

MY very special thanks to 15 people who took time out from their normal schedules to review the draft of this book. This select group has had over 100 years of collective experience in Middle East business affairs and/or backgrounds in international marketing. They made significant suggestions for the content of this book.

From the United States government:
Peter A. Burleigh, Department of State, formerly Deputy Director of the Office of Arabian Peninsula Affairs and formerly Economic Officer and Chargé d'Affaires, American Embassy in Bahrain; Kathleen Keim, Department of Commerce, Commerce Action Group for the Near East (CAGNE); Charles W. Ervin, International Trade Commission, Washington; Richard P. Burns, Agency for International Development, Near East Bureau, formerly Director of Peace Corps, Muscat, Oman; Dr. Allan R. Gall, Peace Corps, Washington, formerly Director of Peace Corps in Sana, North Yemen.

From the private sector:
Carl H. Burris, formerly Vice President Saudi Arabian Operations; Northrop Corporation; David J. Deering, Vice President, formerly in charge of

Iran Operations, Northrop Corporation; Dr. Ralph C. Morgan, corporate representative in Riyadh, Saudi Arabia, Northrop Corporation; Peter K. Simon, consultant to Saudi Arabia Development Corporation, formerly Vice President of Tecon Corporation (Murchison Group), Saudi Arabia, Iran, Kuwait, and formerly Group Vice President Raymond International, Iraq, Libya, Aden, and Lebanon; C. Harold Corbin, Treasurer of NASMA Limited, Rolling Hills Estates, California (with major business in Saudi Arabia).

From the legal profession:
Benjamin P. Fishburne III, Surrey, Karaski and Morse, Washington, and chairman of American Bar Association's Middle East Law Committee; William Burkes Terry, Jr., staff counsel, Saudi Arabia Operations, Northrop Corporation.

From the academic world:
Dr. James D. Calderwood, a Joseph A. DeBell Professor of Business Economics and International Trade, Graduate School of Business, University of Southern California; Dr. Irene L. Lange, chairperson of Department of Marketing and Professor of International Marketing, California State University at Fullerton; Dr. Feliksas Palubinskas, Director of International Business Center and Professor of Marketing, California State University at Long Beach.

Each of you responded to my unreasonable request in a most gracious manner. Thank you.

Quentin W. Fleming

Contents

THE ARABIAN PENINSULA

THE EIGHT NATIONS OF THE ARABIAN PENINSULA: BAHRAIN, KUWAIT, OMAN, QATAR, SAUDI ARABIA, UNITED ARAB EMIRATES, YEMEN ARAB REPUBLIC, PEOPLE'S DEMOCRATIC REPUBLIC OF YEMEN.

THE UNITED ARAB EMIRATES (UAE)

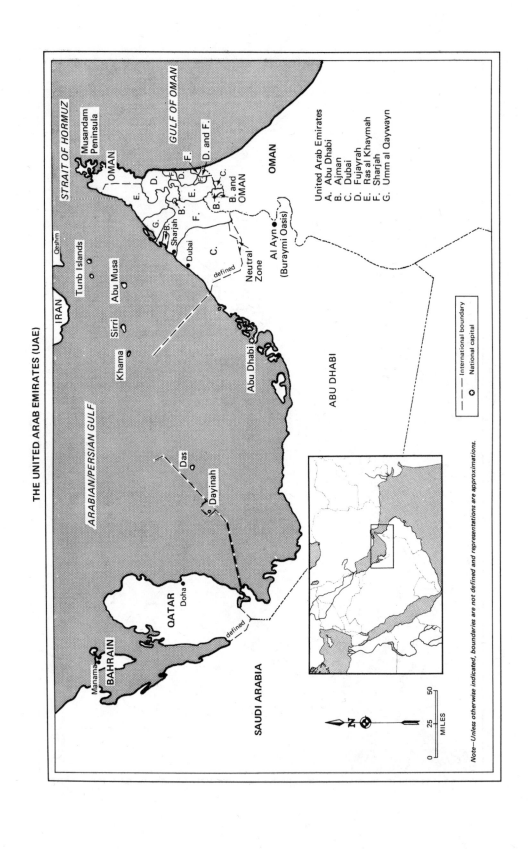

Note—Unless otherwise indicated, boundaries are not defined and representations are approximations.

Introduction

THIS guide to doing business in selected countries of the Middle East is prepared specifically for American businessmen. It is intended to help them do something good for their country and, at the same time, do something good for themselves. In helping their country—which badly needs to have its dollars, petrodollars, recycled into its own coffers—American businessmen should be able to set aside a few dollars for themselves in profits.

You will note that the references above are to "businessmen." These days it is not fashionable to make references to men alone; rather it is common to refer to "men and women" or, better yet, to "persons." But the reference to men alone is quite intentional. The eight countries covered in this book have ancient cultures and are very conservative. Most feel that women have no place in commerce. I accept that view completely, at least for their part of the world, and recommend that you do also. To do otherwise is to invite failure in your commercial undertaking. More on this subject in Chapter 3.

Since the fall of 1973, there has been a new world economic order. At that time, the Western nations paid close to $3 per barrel for crude oil. Today, over seven years later, the price of crude oil has risen over 1,000%. There is no reason to believe it has reached a ceiling. Exactly how high the price will go is completely beyond the control of the Western nations.

Under these circumstances one might expect that demand for imported crude oil would have gone down proportionately. But has it? Absolutely not.

Back in 1973, the United States was importing some 15% of its consumer oil. Today, it is importing about 50%. The result has been a deficit of unprecedented proportions in the United States balance of trade. There is no reason to believe that the deficit will not continue to increase each year.

But those of us who took a basic course in economics a few years back probably remember being told that trade deficits between nations have a way of stabilizing. The first thing that happens is that the currency of the deficit country (in this case, the United States) tends to weaken or go down relative to that of the surplus countries. True. The U.S. dollar *has* taken a beating in comparison with the currencies of the surplus countries since 1973. But is the situation likely to stabilize—that is, will the deficit go down in the future? Not very likely. The reason, again, is that U.S. demand for imported crude oil, instead of going down, has actually increased.

The only other viable way to lower the deficit is for the United States to increase its exports to the oil-producing nations. As Americans, we must be clever and find ways to recycle our own dollars back to ourselves. Also, as American businessmen, we may find it highly profitable to join in this patriotic exercise—the recycling process—and earn a small profit for ourselves as well. The purpose of this book is to assist in this patriotic endeavor.

This study is based on two major premises. The first is that, as we move into the 1980s, the best opportunities for Western business firms to develop *new* clients will not be in the two popular countries of the 1970s, Iran and Saudi Arabia. Although these two nations still possess huge revenues and buying potential, they are highly worked territories. The competition is coming not only from Western business firms but primarily from the highly competitive firms of the Far East (Korea, Taiwan, Japan). In my opinion, the best *new* business opportunities in the 1980s will be in the smaller, lesser-known countries that lie just beyond the borders of the Kingdom of Saudi Arabi: Bahrain, Kuwait, Qatar, Oman, the United Arab Emirates, and the two Yemens. These small nations plus Saudi Arabia will be referred to as the eight target countries.

A second premise of this book is that, in order to effectively pursue business in these small nations, American businessmen must learn something about the Arab culture. In the past, it may have been sufficient to walk into Middle East nations completely ignorant of our customers' backgrounds. But as the years go by and more of the businessmen of these nations attend foreign universities, many of which are in the United States, they become more sophisticated customers. They will not tolerate the insensitivities experienced in the past. Hence the importance of learning something about the Arab culture and the people you hope to be doing business with.

1

Background Information on the Target Countries

Extending southeast from the continent of Asia, almost where it touches Europe, is a large peninsula called Arabia. This land mass contains some of the world's most extreme contrasts. The area is the site of one of the oldest civilizations in recorded history, going back some 6,000 years. Yet in some parts it is the least developed of any in the world today. It contains the richest countries in the world, both in absolute (cash reserve) terms and in per capita terms. Yet it also contains some of the poorest nations and poorest people.

Table 1–1 presents some comparative data on these Arab countries. As a point of reference, data are also shown on England and the United States. The table indicates that all these Arab nations are relatively new in terms of existence as independent states. Even Oman, which was listed as independent since the seventeenth century, was really controlled by Britain until the late 1960s.

All these states are predominantly Arab. But it is doubtful that the Western businessman could see the difference between a nation that is 99% Arab, such as Oman, and one that claims to be only 50% Arab, such as

TABLE 1–1. Comparative statistics on target countries.

	Target Country								Compared with West	
	Bahrain	Kuwait	Oman	Qatar	UAE	North Yemen	South Yemen	Saudi Arabia	England	USA
Date of Independence	1971	1961	17th Century	1971	1971	1918	1967	1932		
Major ethnic divisions	90% Arab	87% Arab	99% Arab	50% Arab 23% Iranian	76% Arab	90% Arab 10% Afro-Arab	99% Arab	90% Arab 10% Afro-Arab		
Literacy	30%	80%	10%	25%	20%	15%	10%	15%		
Area (thousands of square miles)	.2	6	82–115	4	32	75	112	618	94	3,555
Percent of land under cultivation	5%	Less 1%	Less 1%	Less 1%	Less 1%	7%	1%	Less 1%		
Population 1978 (in millions)	.4	1.2	.8	.2	.8	5.1	1.7	7.9	55.9	219.4
GNP—1978 (prelim.—in billions of dollars)	$1.5	$18.0	$2.2	$2.8	$11.4	$3.0	$.7	$63.3	$281.1	$2,117.8
Per capita GNP 1978 (prelim.—in dollars)	$4,100	$14,890	$2,570	$12,740	$14,230	$580	$420	$8,040	$5,030	$9,700

Source: Central Intelligence Agency, *Atlas–Issues in the Middle East,* Washington, D.C.: Government Printing Office, 1973. Population and GNP data from *1979 World Bank Atlas,* Washington, D.C.: World Bank, 1979.

Qatar. Qatar's large population of Iranian descendants could not be differentiated by the Westerner when they are on the street in Arab dress.

Most of these nations have a very low literacy rate. The only exceptions are Bahrain and Kuwait, which have been spending huge sums on education for their populations for several decades. Except for Saudi Arabia, all the nations are small, both in population and in size. None has a significant amount of land under cultivation.

However, once we get into the area of money, these insignificant little nations take on a new dimension. Starting with the oil price increases in 1973, the state of Kuwait has had the highest per capita income of any nation in the world. Following as a close second, and previously in first place, is the United Arab Emirates (UAE). A close third is the small country of Qatar. Thus three of these Arab nations are the richest in the world in per capita terms; and they all surround the Kingdom of Saudi Arabia, which is the very richest nation in the world in absolute (cash reserve) terms.

Even the four other target countries—Bahrain, Oman, and the Yemens—have significance to the businessman by virtue of their location next to these very wealthy nations. Oman has oil reserves and possible additional untapped oil deposits. North Yemen is getting strong financial support from Saudi Arabia. South Yemen, a Marxist state, gets financial assistance from several socialist countries, in addition to outright grants from Arab neighbors. Thus, in terms of being able to pay for Western goods, these target countries clearly have the means.

A country-by-country review follows.

The State of Bahrain

Bahrain (pronounced *Bah*-rain)* consists of several small islands some 15 miles off the coast of Saudi Arabia on the south side of the Arabian (Persian) Gulf.† The largest island; Bahrain, is a flat, sandy land mass 10 miles wide and 30 miles long. The major airport is on the island of Al Muharraq (Moo-*har*-rick), which is connected to Bahrain by a causeway. A 22-mile causeway connecting Bahrain with Saudia Arabia is scheduled for completion in about 1984. The summers are extremely hot and humid, but the winters are quite pleasant.

*Where word pronunciations are shown, accented syllables appear in italics. If no syllable is italicized, emphasis is distributed equally among the syllables.

†The term "Persian Gulf," commonly used in the West, is offensive in Arab countries.

The principal city is Manama (Mah-*nam*-ah) with a population of just under 100,000. The population is primarily Islamic and is almost evenly divided between the Sunni sect in the urban centers and the Shia sect in the rural areas. A large part of the population is Persian. There are Roman Catholic and Protestant churches and a small Jewish population. Bahrain was headquarters for the British Political Agent (a pseudo-ambassador used in undeveloped areas) when Great Britain dominated the Gulf area, so English is widely spoken in most locations. Bahrain is the most modern, most progressive, and most Westernized of all the nations of the Arabian Peninsula.

Through recent archeological findings on the island, it has been established that Bahrain was a flourishing commercial center thousands of years ago. Some 2,000 years ago, it was called the island of Tylos; 5,000 years ago it was Dilmun, a part of Mesopotamian history. Both these early populations fell to hostile armies. Some 100,000 large grave mounds were established over a 1,500-year period during the Dilmun and Tylos eras.

Since the eighteenth century the island has been ruled by the Khalifa family, which entered into a protectorate treaty with the British in 1805. The treaty lasted until 1971, when Bahrain became an independent nation. At that time, there was some talk of a union between Qatar and the seven shaikhdoms of the United Arab Emirates, but nothing came of the discussions. From time to time, Iran has laid claim to Bahrain, but without success.

The state is led by a ruler called the Amir, a member of the Khalifa family. In 1973, the Amir approved a constitution that called for a National Assembly; but by 1975 he disbanded that body for an unspecified period. There are no political parties. In spite of the unsuccessful try at a parliamentary type of government, this nation appears politically stable with individual rights fully protected.

Bahrain is perhaps the most modern of Arabian states. The schools are segregated by sex through the college level, but women are allowed a place in commerce—and each night an evening newcast is done on local color television by a woman. Alcohol is available for sale, even to the local population.

Bahrain has a modern airport serving most of the commercial airlines in the area. Seventy-two-hour visas can be obtained quickly at the airport. Hotel space is readily available, but at a high price. Bahrain is developing as the commercial and banking center of the region. The currencies in Bahrain and the United Arab Emirates are interchangeable at a constant rate. U.S. contacts are as follows:

Embassy of the State of Bahrain
2600 Virginia Avenue NW, Suite 715
Washington, DC 20037
Telephone: (202) 342-0741

Bahrain Representative to the United Nations
747 Third Avenue, 19th Floor
New York, NY 10017
Telephone: (212) 751-8805

The Kingdom of Saudi Arabia

Saudi (Sah-oo-di) Arabia is the largest of the countries on the Peninsula. It is roughly one-third the size of the United States, but with vast areas completely uninhabited. Many of the borders with its southern neighbors, the two Yemens and Oman, are not fully defined. Extremely hot temperatures and high humidity exist along the Arabian Gulf to the north and the Red Sea to the west. The central desert is extremely hot, but with little humidity. High coastal plateaus run along the western coast.

Until recent years and the new-found wealth, most of the population was nomadic or seminomadic. Major cities are Riyadh (population 660,000), Jeddah (population 560,000), Mecca (population 250,000), Medina (population 150,000), and Taif and Dammam (population 100,000). Most of the population is Arab and of the Islamic faith.

Ancient history goes back some 5,000 years along the northern coast. Modern history is influenced by the late King Abdul Aziz ibn Saud (Sahood), who was inappropriately called Ibn Saud by the British. From 1902 to 1932, the great king fought for the unification of the land; and in 1932 all regions were brought together as the Kingdom of Saudi Arabia. Oil was discovered in the northeastern regions in the 1930s and has had a profound effect on the country.

The nation is run by the royal family, most of whom are direct descendants of Abdul Aziz, who was reported to have had over 200 wives and some 42 sons in his lifetime.[1]

As the home of the Islamic religion, Saudi Arabia has assumed the role of guardian and protector of the faith. Life exists in strict accordance with

---

[1]David Howarth, *The Desert King: A Life of Ibn Saud*, Beirut: Continental Publications, n.d., pp. 36, 127, 232. Same title previously printed by Collins, London, 1964.

the dogma of Islam. The faithful pray toward Mecca five times each day, women are concealed from everyone except immediate family, and no alcohol is permitted. The Islamic religion has a major influence over all political and administrative decisions. There are no political parties in the kingdom. Crimes are punished as prescribed in the Koran.

International flights arrive at any of three cities: Jeddah on the west coast, Dhahran on the east coast, and the capital of Riyadh, near the nation's center. Travelers must have a visa, and it is always advisable to have a contact meet you at the airport. Baggage will be closely searched, and no alcohol or pornographic material is allowed. Contacts in the United States are:

> Embassy of Saudi Arabia (temporary address)
> 41 E. 42nd Street, Room 315
> New York, NY 10017
> Telephone: (212) 697-9360
>
> Saudi Arabia Consulate General
> 633 Third Avenue
> New York, NY 10017
> Telephone: (212) 752-2740
>
> Saudi Arabia Consulate
> 2223 West Loop South
> Houston, TX 77027
> Telephone: (713) 961-1790

The State of Kuwait

Kuwait (Koo-*wait*) is a small, flat desert country slightly smaller than the state of New Jersey. It borders Iraq on the north and west, Saudi Arabia on the south, and the Arabian Gulf on the east. The principal city is Kuwait City, which serves as capital and major port and has a population of about 700,000. The climate is tropical from May to October, with extreme temperatures of up to 130°F and an uncomfortable humidity of up to 90%. Many wealthy businessmen depart for the summer, leaving the place to "mad dogs and Englishmen." The winter months are moderate and comfortable.

The local people are mainly Arab; Islam is their religion; and their principal language is Arabic. English is their second language and is widely spoken in business settings.

In ancient history, Kuwait sat at the eastern edges of Mesopotamia. During the period 4000–2000 B.C., Kuwait was at the western edges of the region of Dilmun, which extended over to the island of Bahrain. Ruins have been unearthed in Kuwait dating back some 5,000 years.

The modern history of this country is dominated by the British, whose influence goes back to the 1770s. The English offered protection to the Kuwaitis both from pirates and from tribal bands. In 1899, Shaikh* Mubarak signed a treaty with Britain under which Britain gave the small state protection in return for a promise not to give any territory or grants to a foreign power without the consent of England. The British left in 1961 at the request of the government, and Kuwait then became an independent nation. However, many lasting ties exist today between Kuwait and Britain.

The political structure is a constitutional monarchy. The ruling family, the Al Sabah, selects from its members the head of state, called the Amir. The constitution was approved in 1962; but in 1976 the Amir suspended both the National Assembly and portions of the constitution. There are no political parties in Kuwait, but labor unions are authorized under government regulation. The country is one of the more developed on the Gulf and has advanced into a welfare state, but with a free economy. In the summer of 1980, it was announced that a 50-member parliament is to be elected sometime in 1981.

Kuwait is an ultraconservative Islamic nation. The sexes are segregated in social settings, and many women still wear veils in public. Alcohol is prohibited. Many foreigners are seen on the streets, brought in out of necessity to assist in this labor-short nation's development effort. Foreigners receive the benefit of high wages but are not allowed to participate in Kuwait's "cradle to grave" social welfare system.

Kuwait has a modern international airport with nonstop flights to many European cities. The workweek runs from Saturday to Wednesday and half a day on Thursday. Offices are open from about 8:00 A.M. to 1:00 P.M., then close for a long lunch. Some businesses reopen from 4:30 P.M. to 7:00 P.M. Friday is the holy day and all businesses are closed.

There are several modern hotels, but advance reservations are a must. Visas are required from U.S. citizens. Citizens of Britain and most Arab countries do not need a visa, and travelers with outbound tickets may get a transit visa at the airport for up to 72 hours. It is always advisable to secure a visa in advance of arrival. Regulations do change, and 24 hours in an air-

---

*This spelling is used here, instead of the variation "Sheikh," to emphasize that the word is pronounced "Shake," as in milkshake.

port waiting room can discourage any traveler. Visas may be obtained from the Kuwaiti Consulate in New York or the Embassy of Kuwait in Washington.

Embassy of Kuwait
2940 Tilden Street NW
Washington, DC 20008
Telephone: (202) 966-0702

Consulate of the State of Kuwait
801 2nd Avenue
New York, NY 10017
Telephone (212) 687-8285

Kuwait Mission to the United Nations
235 E. 42nd Street
New York, NY 10017
Telephone: (212) 687-8284

The Sultanate of Oman

Oman (*Oh*-mon) lies on the eastern end of the Arabian Peninsula where it touches the Arabian Sea. On the north, it borders the UAE; on the west, Saudi Arabia; and on the south, the People's Democratic Republic of Yemen (South Yemen). The landscape is varied, ranging from desert to mountain to rich vegetation. The coastline near Muscat, the capital with 50,000 people, is rugged and extremely beautiful. Oman is roughtly the size of Kansas—but that is only an estimate, since some of its borders are not set.

Estimates of the population range from a low of 600,000 to a high of 1.5 million. Obviously, no one knows for certain, and the State Department's estimate of 820,000 is most widely accepted. Roughly half the people are nomadic or live in small villages in the interior. Since a large portion of the population is newly arrived from Pakistan, India, and elsewhere, it has been difficult to assess the exact number.

The principal population is Arab, and Islam is their religion. At least three different branches of Islam are practiced, with Ibadi in the majority. Some English is spoken in business circles. The climate from May to October is hot and damp, with temperatures hitting 120°F and a humidity in the 80s. Winters are moderate.

For almost 150 years, until 1650, the Portuguese ruled Oman. After the country expelled the Portuguese, it extended its control from the Pakistani and Iranian coasts down to Zanzibar and the East African coast. In the early nineteenth century, "Muscat and Oman" (its name until 1970) was the most powerful state in Arabia. It made friends with several Western countries, but the only lasting tie was with Britain. The special relationship with England continues today.

For some 38 years, until 1970, the Sultan of Oman ruled the nation for self-aggrandizing purposes and severely restricted its development. There was but one stretch of paved road, and only the Sultan himself was allowed to own a car. In 1970 the Sultan's British-educated son, Qaboos (Gha-*boos*), took over the nation in a peaceful coup. Since that time, Oman has taken some steps toward modernization.

There is no suffrage in Oman, nor is there a constitution, a legislature, political parties, or elected assemblies of any kind. The Sultan has absolute control, serving as prime minister, minister of defense, minister of foreign affairs, commander-in-chief of the armed forces, and head of the police force. All new laws come from the Sultan, and he is the highest judicial power.

Up to 1970, the gates of Muscat closed at sunset; there was no electricity, and all shipments were by pack animals. Even today, after a decade of modern rule, Oman remains one of the more medieval countries of the Arabian Peninsula. Social relationships with the local population of the type possible in other more progressive Arab Gulf states are not likely in this environment.

Oman has a modern airport and several international flights daily. Hotel space is limited, and advance reservations are a must. Even with a reservation, travelers are sometimes stranded and must sleep in a hotel or airport lobby. Business is conducted on a Saturday-to-Wednesday schedule. Liquor may be purchased by expatriates but not by the Muslim population.

Visas are difficult to obtain and a visitor must have a Nonobjection Certificate (NOC), which can be obtained from the Immigration Department through an Omani sponsor. Therefore, a businessman attempting to establish an initial contact in the sultanate must select a local sponsor before making his first trip to the country. (More on local sponsors in Chapter 5.) Visa information may be obtained from the Embassy of Oman in Washington.

Embassy of Oman
2342 Massachusetts Avenue NW
Washington, DC 20008
Telephone: (202) 387-1980

Oman Mission to the United Nations
605 Third Avenue
New York, NY 10016
Telephone: (212) 682-0447

The State of Qatar

Qatar (Gut-ter), a small, flat desert nation, is a peninsula extending a little over 100 miles northward into the Arabian Gulf from the larger Arabian Peninsula. It is roughly the size of Connecticut. The principal city and capital is Doha (Doe-*hah*), with a population of about 100,000. On the south it borders the United Arab Emirates, and some 25 miles off its westerly coast is the modern island nation of Bahrain.

The population is primarily Arab, with a strong Iranian influence. Arabic is the principal language, but English is common in business settings, and some radio and television broadcasts are in English. The climate is similar to Kuwait's: extremely hot in the summer and moderate in the winter.

Some 100 years ago the Amir of Qatar signed a protectorate treaty with Britain, and close ties with that nation remain. Qatar became independent in 1971, when England relinquished its role in the Arabian Gulf. Attempts were made to combine Qatar, Bahrain, and the seven shaikhdoms of the United Arab Emirates into one nation, but an agreement could not be reached. Strong ties still exist among these three nations.

Since 1972, the nation has been led by Shaikh Khalifa, who replaced his cousin in a peaceful coup. The nation runs under a "Basic Law" adopted in 1970, which provides for a bill of rights and an independent judicial system. While the Amir maintains almost absolute rule, he is guided by an advisory council and cabinet, which includes members not from the royal family, Al Thani. Thus the ruler has attempted to give the people of Qatar a sense of participation in the management of the state.

In social terms, Qatar is somewhere between the ultraconservative Saudi Arabia and the modern Bahrain. Women are allowed to drive cars and hold some important office jobs. Local people cannot use liquor, but expatriate employees may receive permission to import liquor for their own use. There are some English-language movie houses.

Qatar has a modern airport, good surface roads, and good communications with the outside world. A 72-hour visa may be obtained at the airport with proof of onward plane reservations. Longer visas may be obtained from its embassy, but a Nonobjection Certificate from a Qatari sponsor is required.

> Embassy of the State of Qatar
> 600 New Hampshire Ave.
> Washington, DC 20037
> Telephone: (202) 338-0111

Qatar Mission to the United Nations
747 Third Ave.
New York, NY 10017
Telephone: (212) 486-9335

United Arab Emirates (UAE)

The United Arab Emirates (Emer-*ritz*) was formed in 1971. It is a loose confederation of seven small shaikhdoms which were known as the "Trucial Coast" and the "Pirates' Coast" in earlier centuries. These seven shaikhdoms and their estimated populations are:

Abu Dhabi (Ah-boo *dha*-bee)	270,000
Dubai (Do-*buy*)	250,000
Sharjah (Shar-*jah*)	110,000
Ras Al Khaimah (*Rahs* Al *Kay*-mah)	60,000
Fujairah (Foo-*jah*-rah)	28,000
Ajman (*Ahg*-mon)	24,000
Umm Al Qaiwain (*Oom* Al *Gha*-win)	18,000

All these figures are estimates, since the transient population of workers from Pakistan and elsewhere makes an exact tally impossible. Workers from the poorer nations have been known to give up their passports just for the opportunity to work in the UAE, the second richest per capita country in the world.

The country is flat desert, barely above sea level. Since the discovery of oil in the late 1960s, the cities of Abu Dhabi and Dubai have undergone extensive development programs. The UAE is roughly the size of Maine.

Most of the independent Shaikhdoms had a protectorate relationship with Britain starting in the 1800s. After their formation as an independent state in 1971, the ruler of Abu Dhabi, the wealthiest shaikhdom, was chosen as President of the UAE. The Shaikh of Dubai, the second wealthiest shaikhdom, was elected Vice President. Other rulers serve on the Supreme Council. In 1976, the defense forces of the various shaikhdoms were brought into a consolidated UAE force. Each year seems to bring the confederation closer to a unified nation.

The UAE has established a series of social welfare programs for local citizens, including free medical and hospital care, free education, and some free housing. Soaring inflation is taking its share of the new wealth, however. Foreigners in the UAE's larger cities may buy liquor for their own use, and women may work in nonteaching positions. One city has a gambling casino.

The four largest cities have modern international airports. All the emirates are linked by paved roads. Modern hotels exist in most cities, but the cost per day is the highest in the world, as one would expect.

Three-day visas are *sometimes* available at the airport, with proof of valid onward flight tickets and proof of a valid business interest. However, it is prudent to obtain an advance visa from the UAE Embassy in Washington.

United Arab Emirates Embassy
600 New Hampshire Ave. NW
Suite 740
Washington, DC 20037
Telephone: (202) 338-6500

UAE Mission to the United Nations
747 Third Ave.
New York, NY 10017
Telephone: (212) 371-0480

Yemen Arab Republic
(North Yemen; Sana Yemen)

North Yemen lies in the southwestern corner of the Arabian Peninsula with the Red Sea to the west. On the north, it borders Saudi Arabia; on the east, South Yemen. It has three topographical areas: the Tihama, a wide coastal plain some 30 to 60 miles wide; the Highlands, which rise from the Tihama to heights of 12,000 feet; and the Eastern Slopes, which decline from the Highlands to the Empty Quarter of the Arabian Peninsula. It is about the size of Nebraska.

Most Yemenis live in small villages or tribes, in contrast to most other peoples of the Peninsula, who are nomads or seminomads. They are mainly of Semitic origin, but negroid strains exist in the population.

The principal town and capital is Sana (*Sah*-nah), which is located at 7,000 feet in the Highlands and has a population of about 150,000. Climate varies with altitude, but along the coast it is hot and humid. Some English is spoken in business settings.

North Yemen has an ancient history, only part of which has been fully explored. Archeological activity has been limited thus far, perhaps because of the isolated locations. It is believed that the land had civilizations going back several thousand years. From 750 to 150 B.C., it was called Saba (or Sheba), the home of the biblical Queen of Sheba.

Modern North Yemen has witnessed a series of struggles for control of the nation. In 1971, a constitution was adopted and the first nationwide elections took place. An assembly of 159 members was elected; but in 1974 the constitution was temporarily suspended. No political parties exist in the modern sense of the word. The country's legal system is a cross between Islamic and tribal law. A man's testimony is equal to that of two women in the courts.

Women are isolated from the public; and the higher the family rank, the more severe the isolation. Parents arrange marriages for their children, and marriage is more a family affair than a personal activity.

Alcohol is strictly prohibited to the local public. But starting at about 3:00 P.M. each day, and perhaps lasting several hours, local men will get together to chew Qat (pronounced Ghat), a mildly narcotic leaf grown locally. The leaves of Qat are placed in the corner of the mouth and chewed somewhat like tobacco. Much social exchange and business takes place in these meetings. As a businessman, you may be invited to chew Qat; but as a foreigner you can decline if you so choose.

Sana has a small, modern airport which receives flights from Cairo, Jeddah, and Damascus. Hotel space is limited. Visas may be obtained from the YAR Embassy in Washington.

> Embassy of Yemen
> 600 New Hampshire Ave. NW
> Suite 860
> Washington, DC 20037
> Telephone: (202) 965-4760)

> YAR Mission to the United Nations
> 211 East 43rd Street, Suite 1904
> New York, NY 10017
> Telephone: (212) 355-1730

People's Democratic Republic of Yemen
(South Yemen; Aden Yemen)

South Yemen lies on the southern tip of the Arabian Peninsula, at the Gulf of Aden. It borders North Yemen on the northwest, Saudi Arabia on the north, and Oman on the east. The principal city of Aden (*Ah*-den), formerly a British crown colony, has a population of 225,000. It is a fairly modern country with less developed interior regions. The 1,400-square-mile island of Socotra in the Gulf of Aden is also part of South Yemen. The country is about the size of Arizona.

The coasts are sandy and flat and the interior is mountainous. Coastal temperatures are extremely hot, sometimes reaching 130°F. Most of the people are nomadic herders or subsistence farmers. Arabic is the principal language, but English is widely used in business. In the east, several non-Arabic languages are spoken.

South Yemen also has a long history, only part of which is presently known. The land was known as the Minaean, Sabaean, or Himyarite kingdoms as early as 1200 B.C. The area was conquered by the Christian Ethiopians and later by the Persians.

Modern South Yemen was dominated by the British until 1967, when they withdrew. Conflict existed between two leftist groups, each of which attempted to gain power. In 1967, the country was renamed the People's Republic of South Yemen; and in 1970, it changed to its present name. In 1971, a still more radical group assumed power.

South Yemen is governed by a three-man Presidential Council. The country is a Marxist state with ties to the Soviet Union, Cuba, and Ethiopia. Once-close ties to the People's Democratic Republic of China have been strained.

A border war started with North Yemen in 1978, but ended in a truce in 1979. There has been talk of a possible merger of the two Yemens; but with the close relationship of North Yemen to Saudi Arabia, not much is expected from the discussions. Saudi Arabia is adamantly opposed to a Communist form of government and will likely influence North Yemen in such talks.

Since the nation's turn to a Marxist state, women have insisted on an expanded role, including the abandonment of their veils. Although outlawed, Qat is used by the men. Because the city of Aden was under British rule for many years, it has achieved some level of sophistication in comparison with other cities in the Yemens.

Since 1969, the United States has not had diplomatic relations with South Yemen, but that could change at any time since exploratory talks have taken place. For the present, visas for Americans must be obtained through the mission to the United Nations in New York.

> PDR of Yemen Mission to the United Nations
> 413 E. 51st Street
> New York, NY 10022
> Telephone: (212) 752-3066

A Special Note for All First-Time Travelers to the Target Countries

To the experienced traveler in the Middle East (*not* Europe—it isn't the same), much of what follows will be superfluous. But the first-time traveler will find that certain rules are best observed in each of the target countries:

Rule 1—Visa

Obtain a visa in advance in the United States. Do not risk the chance of having to sleep in an airport terminal for a day or so. To obtain the visa, you will need a valid passport, a shot record or a WHO card (see rule 2), passport photos, a check to pay for the visa, and sometimes a local sponsor or Nonobjection Certificate. Rules and regulations do change. Write to the country's embassy in advance. Visas can take two to four weeks to obtain.

Rule 2—Shots

Have a complete set of shots for yourself, with a record on the WHO (World Health Organization) card. Shot requirements will vary, but it is good to have at least cholera, smallpox, yellow fever, and typhoid shots.

Rule 3—Hotel Reservations

Make hotel reservations in advance from a reliable travel agent; pay advance deposits if required.

Rule 4—Contact

Set up a local contact and have the phone number with you when you land. Also, know the phone number of the U.S. Embassy:

> **Bahrain**
> P.O. Box 431, Manama
> Telephone 714151
>
> **Saudi Arabia**
> Palestine Road, Jeddah
> Telephone 65394/5
>
> **Kuwait**
> P.O. Box 77, Kuwait City
> Telephone 424156/8

Oman
P.O. Box 966, Muscat
Telephone 722021

Qatar
P.O. Box 2399, Doha
Telephone 87701/2/3

UAE: Abu Dhabi, Shaikh Khalid Bldg.
Corniche Road, P.O. Box 4009
Telephone 61534/35

Dubai, Al Futtaim Bldg.
Creek Road, Deira, P.O. Box 5343
Telephone 29003

North Yemen
Box 1088, Sana
Telephone 5826,2790

South Yemen
None. Contact British Embassy in Aden.

Rule 5—Local Holidays

Each of these countries celebrates one or two special holidays each year (such as National Day or Independence Day). The exact dates vary from country to country, and it is best to check with the country's embassy before starting out. In addition to these unique holidays, all the nations of the Peninsula honor at least five religious events each year. The dates change yearly, since the Islamic calendar is 11 days shorter than our calendar. Shown below are the five holidays and the Muslim New Year, and the *approximate* dates in 1981:

Prophet's Birthday	19 January
Laitat Al Miraj—Ascension of the Prophet	1 June
Month of Ramadan	3 July to 1 August
Eid Al Fitr—Feast	2 August to 8 August
Eid Al Adha—Feast of the Sacrifice, Haj or Pilgrimage	9 October to 12 October
Hijriyah—Start of Muslim Year 1402	30 October

Businesses are often closed during these periods. Check with the embassy.

Rule 6—Working Hours

Working hours vary from country to country and with different types of businesses. Nevertheless, a pattern is generally followed. Almost everything is closed on Friday, the holy day. An exception is that shops are sometimes open Friday mornings. The normal workweek runs from Saturday to Wednesday. Some offices are open half a day on Thursday. Government offices are usually open only for about five hours in the morning and close about 1:00 P.M. Shops and offices generally open for four hours in the morning, close for a long lunch from noon until 4:30 P.M., then open again for three hours. The American embassies are generally open for about six hours straight through, five days a week (Saturday to Wednesday). The only way to know for sure is to ask in advance of your trip.

Rule 7—Passport Pictures

Always carry a supply of at least a dozen passport photos. You will need them at the most unlikely times and places.

Rule 8—Liquor

Forget about alcohol while you are in these countries, unless it is offered to you by your host, or is perhaps legal for foreigners. Do not try to sneak in a bottle. People go to jail for such violations.

Rule 9—Pornographic Material

Leave the *Playboy* magazines at home. If they are found in your luggage, they are likely to be declared pornographic and taken from you.

Rule 10—Be Patient

Plan for at least a 100% loss of time. Allow a week in the Middle East for what you could accomplish in Chicago in two days. But relax. It is their country, and you are but a visitor seeking their business.

2

How and Where to Find Information: From Your Home – From the Field

THERE is a great deal of information available on the eight target countries: some good, some marginal; some expensive, some free. You can obtain much of the information without leaving the comfort of your own home. For the rest, you will generally find that face-to-face contact produces the best results.

Below is a list of information sources that the Western businessman should find particularly valuable. First are listed those items available from the government.

Department of Commerce

Probably the most extensive, reliable, and inexpensive source of data is that provided by the Department of Commerce. It is headquartered in

Washington, D.C., and has a special group set up to review the Middle East marketplace. This organization, called CAGNE (Commerce Action Group for the Near East), serves as the focal point for the department's study of opportunities in the Near East and North Africa. CAGNE may be reached by writing:

> Department of Commerce
> CAGNE, Room 3202
> Washington, DC 20230
> Telephone: (202) 377-5767

In addition, the Commerce Department operates 61 district offices in 43 states across the nation. These smaller offices have most Commerce Department publications available for purchase and also offer advice to the businessman. The addresses of the local offices are shown in most Department of Commerce publications, or they may be obtained from telephone information. Publications of particular significance include:

1. *A Business Guide to the Near East and North Africa.* Updated about every two years, this guide contains a wealth of information for the prospective businessman. February 1980, price $2.20 (89 pages).

2. *An Introduction to Contract Procedures in the Near East and North Africa.* This report provides information on contract law and practices in 17 Near and Middle East countries, including all the target countries except South Yemen. February 1978, price $2.20 (80 pages).

3. *Overseas Business Reports.* These are special reports published by CAGNE based on information provided by U.S. embassies overseas. Reports of particular interest are:

> *Marketing in Kuwait, OBR 79-18.* June 1979 ($1.25).
> *Marketing in the United Arab Emirates, OBR 77-64.* December 1977 ($.50).
> *Marketing in Saudi Arabia, OBR 79-40.* December 1979 (1.25).
> *Near East / North Africa Business Costs, OBR 79-19.* July 1979 ($.50).
> *World Trade Outlook for Near East and North Africa, OBR 79-09.* April 1979 ($.80).

4. *Foreign Economic Trends and Their Implications for the United States.* These are special reports prepared by the American embassies in various countries and released by the Department of Commerce. Reports are updated roughly each year or whenever new data become available:

> *Bahrain, FET 79-101.* September 1979 ($.50).
> *Kuwait, FET 79-107.* October 1979 ($.50).

Oman, FET 79-044. March 1979 ($.50).
Qatar, FET 79-106. September 1979 ($.50).
Saudi Arabia, FET 80-054. June 1980 ($.50.)
United Arab Emirates, FET 79-085. August 1979 ($.50).
Yemen Arab Republic, FET 79-041. April 1979 ($.50).

5. *Other Special Publications.* The Department of Commerce publishes an extensive series of special brochures designed to assist the businessman. A brief sample is listed below. The titles indicate the nature of the material.

> *Export Information Services for U.S. Business Firms*
> *Export Opportunities for American Business Through the International Development Bank*
> *Export Services of the Bureau of International Commerce*
> *A Guide to Financing Exports*
> *Export Contact List Services*
> *A Research Staff for $34 a Year*
> *The Agent/Distributor Service*
> *Official U.S. and International Financing Institutions*
> *The EMC—Your Export Department*
> *A Basic Guide to Exporting*

Note: Because the United States does not have diplomatic relations with South Yemen, no publications on that nation are available from Commerce, which obtains most of its data from U.S. embassies overseas. The situation could change rapidly with the exchange of diplomatic missions between the two countries.

Government Printing Office (GPO)
Superintendent of Documents

The GPO is the repository of all federal publications, including the documents published by the Department of Commerce. In the case of Commerce, however, it is more expedient to order directly from that agency. Most other federal documents may be ordered from:

> U.S. Government Printing Office
> Superintendent of Documents
> Washington, DC 20402

Publications of particular interest include:

1. *Department of State—Background Notes*
   Bahrain, S/N 044-000-91183-3.
   Kuwait, S/N 044-000-91190-6.
   Oman, S/N 044-000-91129-5.
   Qatar, S/N 044-000-91123-0.
   United Arab Emirates, S/N 044-000-91186-8.
   North Yemen, S/N 044-000-91165-5.
   South Yemen, S/N 044-000-91119-1.
   Saudi Arabia, S/N 044-000-91286-4.

Current updates to these notes run $.80 per copy.

2. *Area Handbooks.* These are comprehensive hardbound books of a high quality prepared for the U.S. government by The American University in Washington, D.C. They have extensive data on selected countries.

☐ *Area Handbook for the Persian Gulf States, S/N 008-020-00682-3.* 1977 ($10.00; 448 pages). Covers Kuwait, Qatar, Oman, the United Arab Emirates, and Bahrain.
☐ *Area Handbook for the Yemens, S/N 008-020-00650-5.* 1977 ($6.00; 266 pages). Data on both North and South Yemen.
☐ *Area Handbook for Saudi Arabia, S/N 008-020-00628-9.* 1977 ($6.30; 389 pages). Data on the kingdom.

Bibliographies on selected subjects are available from the GPO at no charge.

World Bank

While the primary purpose of the World Bank is to provide financial and technical assistance to poorer nations, its staff does perform comprehensive economic research which is available to businessmen. Publications are available free of charge from:

> World Bank
> Publications Unit
> 1818 H Street
> Washington, DC 20433

If you are in a hurry for a given document, include a check for airmail postage. Publications of particular interest include:

☐ *Yemen Arab Republic: Development of Traditional Economy.* January 1979 (303 pages). Current financial data on the country.
☐ *People's Democratic Republic of Yemen: A Review of Economic and Social Development.* March 1979 (169 pages). Data on the country.
☐ *1979 World Bank Atlas* (23 pages). Comparative statistics on 185 countries and territories in the world.
☐ *Catalog of Publications.* A list of all documents available from the World Bank.

Private Sources

Because of the tremendous amount of money flowing into and out of the Middle East, many private publishers have focused attention on that part of the world. A selected sample of ten of the better sources is listed below.

1. *The Businessman's Guide to the Middle East,* by Lillian Africano. This 312-page book, published in 1977, is one of the finest little guides available on the Middle East, at a moderate price. The author, who is from Arab-American parents, stresses the importance of understanding the Arab culture and presents a comprehensive review of 11 nations in the region. The book sells for $12.95 and is available in most bookstores. It may also be purchased directly from:

> Harper & Row, Publishers
> 10 East 53rd Street
> New York, NY 10022

2. *Middle East Annual Review—1980.* Published from London for its sixth year, this review provides 430 pages on issues in the Middle East, covering 25 separate countries, including all the target nations. It has good data, is current, and is moderately priced at $33. Copies may be ordered from:

> The Middle East Review Co. Ltd.
> 21 Gold Street, Saffron Walden
> Essex CB10 IEJ, England
> Telephone: Saffron Walden (0799) 21150

3. *Middle East Year Book—1980.* Also published from London, this reference provides 320 pages of information on 21 countries, including all the

target nations. It is similar to item 2 above, but offers unique coverage and is available for $33 from:

> IC Magazines Limited
> 63 Long Acre
> London WC2E 9JH, England
> Telephone: 01-836-8731

4. *The Middle East and North Africa 1979–80.* Published 26 times since 1948, this high-quality 975-page volume contains a general survey of topical events and country-by-country data. It may be purchased for $74.20 from:

> Europa Publications Ltd.
> 18 Bedford Square
> London WC1B 3JN, England

5. *Middle East Economic Digest.* This weekly magazine covers regional business, contracts to be let, and news in general. It is a high-quality publication from London that has been quite accurate in its projections.

In addition, the publisher provides a series of special reports from time to time. Most recently it has offered the *Middle East Financial Directory— 1980*, for $30. Requests for annual subscriptions to the digest ($250), which are sent airmail, should be addressed to:

> MEED Sales Department
> 21 John Street
> London WC1N 2BP, England

6. *Saudi Business & Arab Economic Report.* This weekly magazine focuses primarily on commerce in the kingdom, but it also offers articles of general interest in the Arab world. A must publication for firms desiring entry or expansion in Saudi Arabia commerce. For an annual subscription ($100), sent airmail, write to:

> *Saudi Business & Arab Economic Report*
> 2100 West Loop South, Suite 1650
> Houston, TX 77027
> Telephone: (713) 961-0245

7. *Mideast Business Exchange.* This monthly magazine covers business and economic issues in the Middle East. Yearly subscription charge is $25. Also available is the *Mideast Business Guide*, a comprehensive guide to 21 countries, including the target nations. It provides names and addresses of po-

tential contacts in the area. The guide emphasizes the need to understand the cultural environment in the Middle East (price $12.00). Both publications may be ordered from:

> Mideast Business Exchange
> 2007 Wilshire Blvd., Suite 900
> Los Angeles, CA 90057
> Telephone: (213) 483-5111

8. *Doing Business.* This series by the international accounting firm of Price Waterhouse provides useful information on starting a business relationship in selected countries, including Kuwait, Oman, Saudi Arabia, and the United Arab Emirates. Copies are available at no cost with a written request to:

> Ms. Josephine Flaccus
> Price Waterhouse
> 1251 Avenue of the Americas
> New York, NY 10020

9. *Doing Business in Saudi Arabia and the Arab Gulf States,* by Dr. Nancy A. Shilling. This comprehensive treatise on Saudi Arabia and five other Gulf states (Bahrain, Kuwait, Oman, Qatar, and the UAE) is probably the most complete single source on the Arabian Peninsula available to businessmen. It is expensive: $185 for the initial 1975 work and $65 for yearly updates. A five-year prepaid supplement series is available for $250. It is unavailable in most public or university libraries, probably because of its price. But if you want one of the best, this book is a must.

Also available from Inter-Crescent, formerly from New York, is a series of reports to assist the businessman in the Arab marketplace. A few examples: *A Practical Guide to Living and Travel in the Arab World,* 1978, price $35; *Marketing in the Arab World* (Social Report), 1980, price $25; *Arab Markets—1979–80* (second edition), price $65; *A Practical Guide to Arabic for the Businessman,* 1978, price $100.

Again, because of the cost, these reports must usually be ordered from the publisher. (They will send a list of publications at no cost.)

> Inter-Crescent Publishing
> P.O. Box 8481
> Dallas, TX 75205
> Telephone: (214) 363-6645
> Telex 732-341 Polser

10. *The Arab Business Yearbook 1980*. First published in 1976, this high-quality volume from London covers 20 countries, including the target nations. It provides data by economic information, financial information, banking, corporate and personal taxation, foreign investment regulations, customs, tariffs, contract law, labor/employment regulations, and development plans. This 500-page volume is available for $43 from Graham and Trotman Ltd., London.

In addition, this publisher has available a series of high quality—but expensive—books on Middle East business. A few samples: *Business Law and Practices Series*, with volumes on Bahrain, Oman, Qatar, Saudi Arabia, and Yemen Arab Republic, all prepared in 1979 by Shair Management Services, price for each volume $275; *Business Laws of Kuwait* (1980) and *Business Laws of Saudi Arabia* (1980), translated by N.H. Karam, price for each volume $297; *Business Laws of the United Arab Emirates* (1980), translated by Dr. M. F. Hall, price $297; *Contract Law in Saudi Arabia and the Gulf States* (1980), N. F. Coulson, 200 pages, price $55; and several other volumes.

A complete listing may be obtained by writing to the publisher at the following address:

> Graham and Trotman Ltd.
> Bond Street House
> 14 Clifford Street
> London W1X 1RD, England
> Telephone 01-493-6351
> Telex 298878 Tomash G

American-Arab Trade Associations

There are several American-Arab trade associations in the United States which can be of value to you in establishing a first contact and which can provide current information on their nation.

> United States-Arab Chamber of Commerce
> One World Trade Center, Suite 4657
> New York, NY 10048
> Telephone: (212) 432-0655
>
> United States-Arab Chamber of Commerce
> (Mid-Atlantic Chapter)
> 1819 H. Street NW, Room 470
> Washington, DC 20006
> Telephone: (202) 293-6975

United States-Arab Chamber of Commerce
(Pacific Chapter)
433 California Street, Suite 920
San Francisco, CA 94104
Telephone: (415) 397-5663 in San Francisco
              (213) 796-5899 in Los Angeles

American-Arab Association of Commerce and Industry
342 Madison Avenue, Suite 1060
New York, NY 10017
Telephone: (212) 986-7229

American-Arab Chamber of Commerce
319 World Trade Building
Houston, TX 77002
Telephone: (713) 222-6152

Mid-American-Arab Chamber of Commerce, Inc.
136 South LaSalle Street, Suite 2050
Chicago, IL 60603
Telephone: (312) 782-4654

Field Contacts

When soliciting information from strangers, it is often more productive to meet in person with the people who have the material. There is always a time delay in publishing data; also, much valuable information never gets published for various reasons. Even people in official positions, if approached properly, may volunteer extremely valuable information on an unofficial basis (for example, "Personally I'd never do business with that individual.") This kind of information just is not available in published works.

Domestically, Washington, D.C., is the most centralized source for data on the target nations. The Department of Commerce is located there, with its CAGNE staff and other advisers on doing business overseas. The State Department, despite its size and wealth of data, is not likely to provide much help to a private firm. However, you may find a recently returned embassy official in the State Department offices who can provide you with valuable insights and suggestions for further action. The World Bank has its headquarters in downtown Washington, as does the U.S.-Arab Chamber of Commerce branch mentioned above. All the target nations except South Yemen have an embassy in Washington. Frequently, foreign embassy personnel will be of great help and will talk more freely about their country in person than they would by written correspondence. This is not always the case, however, since Gulf embassies are frequently short-staffed.

In New York City, all target nations, including South Yemen, have mission offices to the United Nations. Addresses of these offices are given in Chapter 1. In addition, there are two U.S.-Arab trade organizations in New York, as mentioned above.

Overseas, there is a wealth of information available to you. All U.S. embassies have commercial or economic officers whose job it is to study the local business environment. These professionals can be extremely useful. Embassies of the other nations, particularly the British embassies, are also worth contacting. Depending on how you approach them, they can be as valuable to you as the U.S. embassies.

Finally, the local population can be contacted directly for assistance. Banks in each of the target countries are always close to the business community. Each nation has a chamber of commerce to assist businessmen. Each local government has a ministry devoted to commerce, but the titles vary. As a starting point, check with the U.S. embassy in each nation for suggestions on your best government and private business contacts.

In summary, it is up to you to make your own field contacts and to screen the objective, valid information from the biased recommendations you are certain to receive. Six groups of potential contacts are included in this guidebook:

- Foreign embassies, UN missions, and their addresses (given by target nation in Chapter 1).
- U.S. embassies and addresses by target country (given in Chapter 1).
- American-Arab chambers of commerce in the United States (given earlier in this chapter).
- Local chambers of commerce by target country (given at the end of Chapter 6).
- Local American (or British) banks in the target countries (see Appendix A).
- A list of government ministries by country (see Appendix B). *Note*: You should not approach government ministries until you have made contact with the commercial or economic officer in the U.S. Embassy.

Good hunting.

3

The Arab Culture:
A Brief Overview

IDEALLY, the American businessman wanting to fully learn about his future Arab customers would set out in three simultaneous directions: he would learn the Arabic language; he would convert to the Islamic religion; and he would move into an Arab ghetto to learn from the people. This effort could take years and is obviously impossible from a practical sense. Thus, in attempting to learn about the Arab culture, the businessman must settle for something less than an ideal approach.

The Arabic language is a very difficult one to learn; the sounds do not come easily to a native English speaker. In a "saturated" environment, you might pick up the language in a year. But who can spare a year? And who can find an Arab environment in which to saturate himself?

Because the Arab people are close to their religion, probably as much as any people in the world, no understanding of the culture can come without some understanding of the religion. In the Arab world, Islam permeates everything social, political, and legal. Therefore, prerequisite to knowing the Arab is to know something about Islam, his religion.

This chapter has two goals. First, it presents a brief glimpse of the Arab culture in the hope that the reader will want to learn more about it, either by undertaking additional readings or by closely observing the Arab people when he makes contact with them. A suggested list of initial readings is included at the end of the chapter. Second, and perhaps more important from a practical sense, this chapter points out the *no-no's* in the Arab world, so that initial contacts are not impaired by avoidable and costly mistakes. Perhaps a good starting point is to illustrate a mistake made by a well-known nonfiction writer—the kind of mistake that need not happen with a little preparation.

The writer Anthony Sampson has published such books as *The Sovereign State, The Secret History of ITT; The Arms Bazaar;* and *Anatomy of Britain.* In 1975, he published a book entitled *The Seven Sisters,* a documentary dealing with the seven largest oil companies. Like most successful nonfiction writers, Sampson did a considerable amount of research before publishing his book. In his introduction, he mentions the places he visited and the people he interviewed: "In Bahrain I talked to Yusaf Shirwa, the oil minister, and Ben Mubarak, the foreign minister."[1] Luckily for Sampson, he wasn't dependent on the foreign minister in Bahrain for future business. For even though His Excellency has a good sense of humor, Sampson committed a rather "dumb" mistake—a mistake that would have cost an eager businessman any future contacts with this ministry.

I had the honor of meeting the foreign minister of Bahrain a few years back. But at that time he was not called "Ben Mubarak." Rather, his proper full name was Shaikh Mohammad bin Mubarak Al Khalifa. His given name was Mohammad. Bin Mubarak indicated he was from Mubarak, or the son of Mubarak. Bin or ibn can be used interchangeably. If there had been a second bin after bin Mubarak, it would have indicated the name of his grandfather, for example, bin Hamad. The last part, Al Khalifa, signifies that he is from the Khalifa family, which is the royal family of Bahrain. The foreign minister of Bahrain should properly have been referred to as "Shaikh Mohammad." Under no circumstances should he have been called "Ben Mubarak" (as in Benjamin), for that is not his name. Such improper usage merely signifies a lack of interest in or knowledge of the culture.

In Bahrain "Shaikh" indicates a member of the royal family. In Saudi Arabia it can be used simply as a title, like Duke or Earl, as is the case with Shaikh Yamani, the well-known oil minister.

[1]Anthony Sampson, *The Seven Sisters,* London: Hodder and Stoughton, 1975, p. xiv.

Religion

Islam is one of the great major religions of the world. It has in excess of 750 million followers, called Muslims. Yet it is probably the least understood religion in the Western world.

Islam (meaning "submission to God") is the third major religion to develop in the Middle East. It builds on Judaism and Christianity in that it too worships one God (Allah is Arabic for God). Followers of Islam feel that Abraham, Moses, and Jesus (Ibrihim, Musa, and Isa) were but a series of prophets, the last and greatest of whom was the Prophet Mohammed. It is believed that Mohammed received the final and complete word from God, revealed to him through the Angel Gabriel and resulting in the Koran (Quran), the Muslim holy book.

Thus the Koran reflects the word of God, and its impact on the Arab people cannot be overemphasized. Passages from the Koran are frequently quoted in ordinary conversation among the rich and poor, in cities and in villages, and among the wandering Bedouin. The Koran is incorporated into prayers five times each day. It is the basis for the Islamic legal system; and a drift too far away from religious precept can topple even powerful governments, as it did in Iran and Pakistan.

Each Muslim has five primary duties, called the five pillars of Islam:

1. The profession of faith, which consists in repeating in one's prayers, "There is no God but God, and Mohammed is the Messenger of God." This saying is inscribed in Arabic on the flag of Saudi Arabia.
2. Prayers five times a day: before dawn, at midday, in the late afternoon, at sunset, and in the evening. Worshippers prostrate themselves in the direction of the House of God in Mecca, Saudi Arabia.
3. Alms-giving, or the gift of money from the rich to the poor.
4. Fasting during the ninth Muslim month of Ramadan. Believers are enjoined from eating, drinking, smoking, or having sexual intercourse during the daylight hours.
5. The Pilgrimage (or Haj) to the Holy City of Mecca during the twelfth Muslim month.

The Muslim calendar, which in 1981 recorded the year 1402, began in the year 622 A.D. with the flight of Mohammed from Mecca to Medina. The calendar is almost exclusively used on the Arabian Peninsula today and reflects the lunar year—that is, 354 days, divided into 12 months. The Gregorian calendar, our calendar, is not used to any extent in either business or government offices. Thus a "two-month visa" is good only 56 days!

After the death of Mohammed, in 632 A.D., the question of his successor arose. The outcome resulted in a religious breach. The majority of Muslims believe that Mohammed's successor was elected. These people are referred to as Sunni (*Soon*-e) Muslims. The minority held that the successor was Ali, Mohammed's son-in-law and cousin. These people are referred to as Shia (*She*-ah) Muslims and are a minority in Islam, but hold a majority of the populations in Iraq and Iran and a bare majority in Bahrain and North Yemen. There are additional minor Muslim sects, for example the Ibadi in Oman, but the Sunni and Shia represent the majority of Islamic people.

One last word about religion. Not every Arab is a Muslim; some are Christians and some follow other religions. But most of the people you will meet on the Arabian Peninsula will be of the Islamic faith.

Language

Second to religion in understanding the Arab people is a knowledge of the language. While it is impractical for the businessman to learn Arabic, it is highly recommended that you learn something about the language.

Arabic is another thread that links all Arab peoples. Although there are many different dialects, a Gulf Arab can be understood in Casablanca, Tunis, Cairo, Sana, or any Arabic-speaking setting.

Arabic is a flowing, poetic language. Gestures, shouting, touching, and emotions are an indispensable part of the communication process. It often seems, and perhaps it is true, that two or more Arabs can communicate nicely with everyone talking at the same time.

Short vowels are usually not used in written Arabic. While much debate goes on in English as to the proper spelling of Jeddah, or Jiddah, or Juddah, the Arabs solve it with three letters: JDH. Arabic is, therefore, an ideal type of shorthand. Arabic has certain sounds that do not exist in English. By the same token, certain English sounds do not exist in Arabic (the p, for example—often you will hear an Arab ask for a "Bebsi Cola").

It is said that much is lost in translation from Arabic to English. So when you see two slightly different versions of the same paragraph from the Koran, both are probably correct. Each translation is approximate at best. What is really missing in the English version is the emotion of the Arabic.

Perhaps a quote can best illustrate the important differences: "We must be patient with the Arab in discussion; he is intellectually incapable of coming directly to the point."[2] This quote does not reflect on the intelligence of the Arab; rather, it is an illustration of how the Arabic language does not permit the Arab to make his point quickly. He will come to the point, after a fashion. Herein lies a message for the Western businessman.

One last point. While it is impractical to try to learn the Arabic language, you should make a concerted effort to correctly pronounce certain key names—the country and city you will visit, your host's name, and so on. I know people who lived in Dhahran, Saudi Arabia, for five years, yet they continue to pronounce that location in three syllables: "Dha-ha-ron." Obviously, they never listened to local people pronounce the name; or perhaps they never met any local people in five years. Most likely, they fraternized only with other Americans. But if they had taken just a moment they would have heard local people pronounce the city with two syllables only: *"Dha-ron"* or more properly *"Dhah-ron."*

Before you make an important business contact, take a moment and learn how to pronounce his name correctly. Ask your interpreter or someone who speaks the language. Before you visit Shaikh Ahmed, remember that Shaikh is pronounced "Shake" and that Ahmed has two syllables: *"Ah-med."* Of course, if all else fails and you are visiting a high government official, you are always on safe ground by saying "Your Excellency."

Women

Another important part of appreciating the Arab culture is to have some understanding of the role of women in Arab life. Today, in the Arab world, the status of women varies greatly among the more liberal countries (Lebanon, Egypt, Syria) and the more traditional states. Six of the eight target countries are in the more traditional category, but even among the six states there are differences in the role of women—between, for example, Abu Dhabi and Saudi Arabia.

The status of Arab women is a sensitive subject to the traditional Arab. He feels it is not something that should be open to public discussion. In the Western world, women have a different role than they do in Arab nations—a role that is changing almost daily. So while you must learn to adapt to the changing role of women in your own environment, you must also understand how Arabs perceive women in order to appreciate their culture.

[2]John Laffin, *The Arab Mind—A Need for Understanding*, New York: Taplinger Publishing Company, 1975, p. 82.

Since the Muslim religion has a profound effect on all Arabs, the traditional ones in particular, perhaps a starting point is the Koran itself. The following are quotes from the Koran, as translated by N. J. Dawood, a man born in Iraq and educated in England. The traditional chapter (sura) and verse are also indicated.

SURA 2:223   Women are your fields: go, then, into your fields as you please.

SURA 2:228   Women shall with justice have rights similar to those exercised against them, although men have a status above women.

SURA 4:34   Men have authority over women because Allah has made one superior to the others, and because they spend their wealth to maintain them. Good women are obedient. They guard their unseen parts because Allah has guarded them. As for those from whom you fear disobedience, admonish them and send them to beds apart and beat them. Then if they obey you, take no further action against them.

SURA 24:31   Enjoin believing women to turn their eyes away from temptation and to preserve their chastity; to cover their adornments, except such as are naturally displayed; to draw their veils over their bosoms and not to reveal their finery except to their husbands, their husband's fathers, their sons, their stepsons. . . .

SURA 33:51   You may put off any of your wives you please and take to your bed any of them you please. Nor is it unlawful for you to receive any of these whom you have temporarily set aside. That is more proper, so that they may be contented and not vexed, and may all be pleased with what you give them.

SURA 4:11   A male shall inherit twice as much as a female.

SURA 2:282   Call in two male witnesses from among you, but if two men cannot be found, then one man and two women whom you judge fit to act as a witness.[3]

After reviewing these few quotes from the Koran,* and keeping in mind the importance of the Koran to the Arab, you should have little doubt that the traditional Arab businessman views a woman from a different perspective than you do. Then how best to deal with women in these situations?

[3]N. J. Dawood, trans., *The Koran*, Middlesex, Eng.: Penguin Books, 1959.

*It must be mentioned that Arab-Americans have reviewed these quotes and have commented that they are taken out of context and refer to "wives," not "women" in general. Perhaps, although the distinction is difficult for the Westerner to fully understand. The central issue is still that the Westerner and the traditional Arab are likely to perceive the role of women (or wives) in a different way.

The answer is easy: avoid the subject. Do not bring up the subject of women unless your host does. Inquire as to the health of his father or sons, but let him start the discussion of his wife or daughters, if he cares to.

John Laffin, in his book on the Arab culture, describes one of his early experiences:

> When I first traveled in Arab countries, I sometimes took my wife with me to interviews so she could take notes while I concentrated on the conversation. It was useful, too, to be able to compare impressions. We were soon to learn that this practice was a mistake.[4]

Even a professional who has studied and written on the culture can make avoidable mistakes. Laffin offers an explanation for the reaction of his Arab host:

> With my wife present the Arab, no matter how Westernized, was hesitant, evasive, and even hostile. I was exposing him to shame should he be unable to answer a question. In any case, a woman had no business taking part in a conversation between men. Even when my wife sat passively and silently throughout the interview, the tension remained. When I later interviewed the same men alone, the atmosphere was quite different.[5]

Arab homes are intentionally designed with a womens' quarter and a mens' area. The two do not mix, nor do the two paths cross. Men entertain men, and women are with women—period. Even in a modern, Western-educated Arab home—where you can listen to stereo music, pull a *Playboy* magazine from a rack, and perhaps even have a drink of Scotch—you are likely not to meet the mother or wife or sisters of your host. If he chooses to introduce you, so much the better. But do not suggest the introduction yourself. Respect his position.

Why does the traditional Arab feel that women and business do not mix? Many say it is simply the historical role of women as defined in the Koran. An Arab writer, Sayed Kotb, suggests another reason:

> . . . the entry of the Arab woman into the world of business is opposed by traditionalists not on the basis of her abilities or inabilities, but on the assertion that in the world of business a woman could not retain her chastity.[6]

---

[4]John Laffin, *op. cit., p. 103.*
[5]*Ibid.*
[6]Sayed Kotb, *Social Justice in Islam*, translated by John B. Hartie, Washington, D.C.: American Council of Learned Societies, 1953, p. 49.

Undoubtedly, as the years go by, the role of the Arab woman will change. But as a Western businessman, you must keep in mind that your primary goal is to sell your product. This being the case, you cannot afford to campaign for other causes, no matter how just. So leave your wife at home; don't chase the girls in Arab countries, particularly local girls; and take a nonintruding position with respect to the women in your host's family.

Israel

I was over 40 when I first traveled outside the United States. At that time, I moved with my family to the Middle East. After a year or so, a realization came crashing through to me: when Americans do not travel abroad, they do not get a perspective on both sides of the Arab-Israeli question. Without taking a position on the rightness or wrongness of either side, I believe it can safely be said that the American communications media (radio, television, the press, magazines, movies) have made little attempt to be objective on the Arab-Israeli issue. Over the years the media have carefully presented one side only: the Israeli side. As with any issue, there are at least two sides, and each side has many viewpoints, some right and some wrong. The point is that, as an American, you have probably heard only one half of a complex story.

How do you as a businessman respond to this issue? You simply avoid it. As with other controversial political matters, it is risky to get involved or to take positions. The important thing is to recognize that you have been presented with only a limited version of the story by virtue of living in the United States. And both sides have their points. But as a businessman, you need not and should not get involved.

Pride, Face, Shame

There is nothing foreign to the American culture about taking pride in one's work or presenting a good face. What is foreign is the degree to which the Arab will go to save face—even to the extent of experiencing pain. Also, the Arab seems to be motivated by a continual fear of shame in his every action. Such extremes do not exist in the West.

The message for you as a Western businessman is that, when dealing with Arab customers, you must have a sincere respect for the importance of Arab pride. You must take care not to puncture it in any way. You must be prepared to give up something in negotiations, no matter how small, in order for your Arab customer to save face. To win unconditionally in a negotiation, and not to give something to save face, will hurt your enterprise in the long run.

You must not place your customer in a position that could lead him to experience shame, whether real or imagined. If he makes a statement you know to be incorrect, do not correct him in public or in front of others. You must recognize that you are dealing with a very sensitive individual who is motivated by desires and fears that appear extreme by your standards. The more educated the Arab, particularly those educated in the West, the more difficult it will be to observe these differences. But they will be present, and it is important that you be aware of them. Pride, face, and shame are important to your new customers.

Hospitality and Physical Closeness

> The history of nomadic hospitality goes back to biblical times and further. The quoted reward Abraham reaped was given to him by God because of his exceeding hospitality . . . . The hospitality of the Bedouins, the modern-day heirs of Abraham, has been often described. It is a noble trait, exhibited proudly even by the poorest Bedouin, and impressive even in the modified and reduced form in which one encounters it among Arab city folks.[7]

While perhaps no one can trace the origin of Arab hospitality with certainty, no one who has ever visited an Arab home can deny it exists. An Arab feels compelled to invite a visitor to come to his home to dine. The invitation may encompass friends, new acquaintances, and perhaps even adversaries. Even Arabs of very modest means feel compelled to extend the invitation to guests, perhaps at the expense of a family's food supply for the week. The tradition may well be an outgrowth of severe life in the desert, where failure to extend such an invitation could have resulted in the death of the visitors.

Once an invitation is extended by your Arab host, it is extremely important that you accept. To do otherwise could be offensive, even disrespectful, to your host. It is always proper to give the host an out by replying that you

---

[7]Raphael Patai, *The Arab Mind*, New York: Charles Scribner's Sons, 1976, p. 84.

do not want to be a burden. But if the host repeats the invitation for the third time, it is very important that you accept his offer! A modern, Westernized Arab may invite you to a local restaurant instead of his home, but the tradition is the same. In such a case, you should let the host graciously take care of the bill, for he is the one entertaining you.

On entering the Arab home, you may find that your host wants to sit uncomfortably close to you, talk directly into your face, and ask questions that seem personal. Many Americans find these practices difficult to adjust to and somewhat offensive. But great care must be taken not to recoil from your host. He is merely trying to indicate his friendship.

Remember, this is a culture in which it is acceptable for men to walk on the streets holding hands with other men, and for men to kiss each other in greetings or departures. This physical closeness is not an indication of homosexuality, as it might be in the West. Rather, it is an expression of friendship between men. Thus, if your Arab host extends this friendship to you, you should accept it in the spirit of his values and not your own.

Perception of the West

It is likely that your Arab counterpart will perceive you in much the way you will perceive him: as a stereotype. You will feel that all Arab businessmen are rich, ruthless, and selfish, and tend toward excessive gambling, drinking, and outrageous sexual behavior when out of their habitat. You know this because you have seen them in movies and on television, and have read stories about their behavior.

Your counterpart may well see you as the embodiment of all Westerners. Thus you reap the benefits of the British and French and other Europeans whose historical relationship with the Arabs you do not need or want. Modern history is filled with examples of force used on Arab populations in order to further Western political objectives. Nobody needs that kind of help to start a business relationship.

You are also likely to find that the Arabs have great respect and admiration for the West's technology, but an even greater distrust of the West's social values. While they would like to adopt much of the technological improvements, they do not want them if it will result in a change in their traditional values. Hence the Western salesman with his wares runs right into cultural and religious barriers, based on a false perception.

Business Relations

One of the first contrasts the Western businessman will encounter is the routine in the Middle East business office. The Westerner will arrive promptly for an appointment, only to be left waiting in a sparsely furnished outer office for a long time. Once the host invites the eager Westerner into his office, there is yet another barrier: the ritual of coffee and small talk. The Arab host is not anxious to discuss business immediately. Rather, he wants to inquire into the health of your family, the comfort of your trip, the adequacy of your hotel accommodations. He is not being rude; he is merely showing you respect by his standards.

Once the business discussion begins, there are countless interruptions. Phone calls continue to come in. People are constantly knocking at the door, and are admitted by the host. Associates of the host will come in, sit down, and listen to your private(?) business discussion. Such is the routine of a Middle East business office.

For centuries in Middle East commerce it has been commonplace for those who arrange a business deal to get a piece of the action. Their piece of the deal may not be obvious; that is, the value may be buried in the total. Nevertheless, it is there. There is nothing immoral or improper in the arrangement by their standards. It is an accepted part of doing business in the Arab world.

But by Western standards, particularly American standards, these added costs have a sinister connotation: they are bribes, payoffs, kickbacks. Much discussion has taken place on the subject in the United States, to the amazement of Middle Easterners and to the delight of European businessmen. In the United States, there are now laws that prevent such costs in business transactions (for example, the Foreign Corrupt Practices Act of 1977). Thus, as an American businessman, you have the additional burden of keeping such costs out of your business dealings. Your French competitor will not be so encumbered.

In the United States, businessmen pride themselves on their ability to get to the heart of the problem. They are direct. They speak their minds. They say what they mean. Not so in the Middle East. There, businessmen take pride in their indirectness—their ability to spend hours talking without disclosing their true position. This is difficult for the Westerner to understand. As John Laffin stated in his cultural study:

> No foreigner should assume that because an Arab does not say "no" he means "yes." Almost every Arab will avoid a blunt refusal, largely because

it is improper to rebuff people so brusquely. Those Westerners who assume an affirmative in the absence of a negative and then condemn the Arab when they find they are wrong, are doing the Arab an injustice; he does not intend to deceive. . . .[8]

This is perhaps the most difficult message for the Western businessman to learn: in negotiations and in bargaining, do not say what you mean; do not come directly to the point. Talk for hours around the central issue. Many financial scars have resulted from a lack of understanding of this point.

This chapter has attempted to give American businessmen an overview of the Arab culture. But justice cannot possibly be done to the subject. It would take years to properly study this ancient and proud culture. Therefore, the best to hope for is a small appreciation of the most obvious differences between Western and Arab cultures. It is also hoped that the prospective businessman will continue to read and study the backgrounds of his new customers. The game is the same, only the rules and players have been modified. Again, going back to the Laffin study:

> If all this seems trivial I must say again that to apply Western culture values to the Arab world is a mistake. To respect their pride and be aware of their shame works to the foreigner's advantage.[9]

Dos and Don'ts for Foreigners on the Arabian Peninsula

- ☐ Do accept invitations from your Arab host.
- ☐ Do as your host does if you are unsure of yourself.
- ☐ Do remove your shoes at the door of a house if others do.
- ☐ Do shake hands with your host and guests at every chance.
- ☐ Do accept Arabian coffee or tea when offered.
- ☐ Do know how to indicate "no more" Arabian coffee by placing your fingers over the top of your cup (or by shaking the cup back and forth) when returning it.
- ☐ Do stand when people enter a room, except when they are servants or workmen.
- ☐ Do have a businesscard ready to hand to a new acquaintance—ideally, one with Arabic on the reverse side.

[8]John Laffin, *op. cit.*, p. 149.
[9]*Ibid.*, p. 96.

- ☐ Do speak slowly and clearly to your Arab host. His English may appear better than it actually is, and he may have trouble understanding you.
- ☐ Do adopt a patient attitude when transacting business in the Middle East. Be prepared for and accept delays as normal.
- ☐ Don't talk down to your host, no matter how uneducated he may be. He will see through it and resent it.
- ☐ Don't compliment your host on his personal goods to any great extent, or you may force him to offer to give the article to you. To accept or reject his offer of the gift is a "no win" situation for you.
- ☐ Don't eat your food with your left hand, as this is the unclean hand.
- ☐ Don't talk to or stare at Arab women, even if they are staring at you.
- ☐ Don't ask for pork or liquor at meals.
- ☐ Don't cross your legs and show the bottom of your foot to an Arab. It is offensive.
- ☐ Don't give an Arab a "thumbs up" sign; to him it is the same as giving someone the "finger" in the West.
- ☐ In business discussions, don't say things you don't mean or are not prepared to do. In the Arab culture the spoken word, an oral promise, is often more important than a written contract.

Suggested Initial Readings

Rather than provide an exhaustive list of books on Arab culture and history, I have selected what I consider to be the ten best sources of initial readings on the subject, all readily available in most U.S. libraries. (For an expanded bibliography, see Appendix D.)

1. N. J. Dawood, trans., *The Koran*, Middlesex, Eng.: Penguin Books, 1959. (Or any version of the Koran.) The Muslim holy book—the word of Allah as given to Mohammed by the Angel Gabriel—is more important by far to Arab businessmen than is the Bible to Western businessmen. It is an important starting point to understanding this culture.

2. John Laffin, *The Arab Mind—A Need for Understanding*, New York: Taplinger Publishing Company, 1975. An interesting look at Arab culture from a Westerner's perspective. The book is controversial in the Arab world and is felt to be grossly misleading. Nevertheless, it does attempt to explain, from a Westerner's perspective, why Arabs behave as they do. It is easy and interesting reading.

3. Raphael Patai, *The Arab Mind*, New York: Charles Scribner's Sons,

1976. This book bears the same name as Laffin's but has few other similarities. It is longer (376 pages versus 190 pages) and is more penetrating in its analysis of the Arab culture. It is difficult but valuable background reading.

4. *Area Handbook for the Persian Gulf States, Area Handbook for the Yemens,* and *Area Handbook for Saudi Arabia,* Washington, D.C.: Government Printing Office, 1977. These three low-cost volumes, mentioned in Chapter 2, provide an excellent overview of Arab history and some cultural information.

5. Lillian Africano, *The Businessman's Guide to the Middle East,* New York: Harper & Row, 1977. This short guide, also mentioned in Chapter 2, contains some excellent sections on the Arab culture.

6. Marianne Alireza, *At the Drop of a Veil,* Boston: Houghton Mifflin Co., 1971. This is a light-reading true story of an American girl who marries an Arab and moves to the Kingdom of Saudi Arabia. Her experiences give an insight into the contrasts between the two cultures.

7. Geoffrey Bibby, *Looking For Dilmun,* London: Collins, 1970. (Probably out of print, but a "black market" copy with no publisher is available in most Middle East bookstores for about $5.00.) While this narrative lacks the flair of James A. Michener's book, it resembles a true-to-life *The Source.* The author describes excavation which starts on the island of Bahrain and is then extended to Qatar, Kuwait, the UAE, and Saudi Arabia. Evidence of highly developed civilizations going back some 6,000 years is established. It is fascinating background reading on the history of the area.

8. Michael Field, *A Hundred Million Dollars a Day,* London: Sidgwick & Jackson Ltd., 1975. This is an easy-to-read, interesting story of Middle East oil, resulting wealth, and ensuing problems for the newly rich. One of the best books on the subject, it is written by a man who has become London's leading writer on Middle East oil and wealth.

9. David Howarth, *The Desert King: A Life of Ibn Saud,* London: Collins, 1964. (Probably out of print, but available in Middle East bookstores, with no publisher shown, for about $15.00.) This book describes the fascinating life of the founder of Saudi Arabia, King Abdul Aziz ibn Saud (incorrectly referred to in the West as Ibn Saud). Abdul Aziz, who died in 1953, never had more than four wives at a time, in strict obedience to his religion. But through extensive use of divorce, he managed to have more than 200 wives during his lifetime and fathered numerous children. His offspring are now the royal rulers of the Kingdom of Saudi Arabia.

10. H. A. R. Gibb, *Mohammedanism,* New York: Oxford University Press, 1962. The author, Sir Hamilton A. R. Gibb, is considered one of the best authorities on Islam from a Western perspective, and his book is a classic introduction to this normally dry subject. Because religion is so deeply

embedded in the social, legal, and cultural activities of the Arab world, some insight is important if one intends to have an understanding of the culture.

Finally, no matter how well read you are on the subject, or how much exposure you may have had to the Arab culture, remember that your attitude is key. As a former Peace Corps director in an Arab country stated recently:

> "Arab culture" can encompass a wide range of possible behavior, depending on the personality, degree of education, Westernization, and so on of the individual. Statements and do's and don'ts may not be universally applicable in the Gulf, and what is needed most is an awareness that cultural differences and sensitivities do exist.[10]

---

[10]Interview with Richard P. Burns, former Director, Peace Corps Oman, Washington, D.C., November 13, 1979.

4

Contract Laws
and Legal Systems

ALTHOUGH there is a common cultural bond running through all Arab countries, there is nothing resembling a common Arab position on most issues. Each Arab state is likely to have its own position. Likewise, there is no set of laws or legal principles that apply to all Arab states. Each country must be reviewed individually. Only Islamic law, called Sharia law (meaning Islamic jursiprudence), affects all Arab states, but to varying degrees—running from the traditional rules of Sharia law in Saudi Arabia to the codified laws of Bahrain and Kuwait. Even the codified laws have a strong Islamic foundation.

Sharia (Sha-*ree*-ah) law is considered to be created by God, not by man; hence the very strict interpretation of it and resistance to changes by Islamic followers. As a legal system, it has four basic sources:

1. The Koran—the word of God as given to Mohammed by the Angel Gabriel. While the Koran contains some 6,000 religious verses, about 200 are strict legal rules. Example: "Surely they say usury is like sale, but God has made sale lawful and usury unlawful" (Sura 2.275, 276).

2. The Sunna (*Soon*-ah)—the practices and sayings of the prophet Mo-

hammed, what he did or approved of during his lifetime. This could be equated with Islamic common law.

3. The Ijma (*Egh*-mah)—the consensus of the whole community. It is based on the belief that God would not permit all His people to be in error. The consensus can be either from the whole community or from the Imams, the religious leaders of the community.

4. The Qiyas (*Gea*-yas)—the analogies. When a situation appears in which no precedent can be found in the Koran, Sunna, or Ijma (in that order), an analogy is permitted for a solution.

Sharia law is further divided into four schools, each having its influence on a different part of the Islamic world:

1. The Hanafi (Hon-nah-fee) school, founded by Abu Hanifi in Iraq, was adopted by the Ottoman Empire and is still important in those regions once dominated by the Ottomans. Thus parts of western Saudi Arabia and also the eastern shore follow the Hanafi school.

2. The Maliki (Mah-lee-kee) school, based on the practices of the judges in Medina, Saudi Arabia, has its influences today in North Africa, West Africa, upper Egypt, and Kuwait.

3. The Shafii (Sha-fee-ee) school, founded by Shafi, a legal scholar in Arabia from 768 to 820 A.D., has its influence today in lower Egypt and parts of the southwestern corner of the Arabian Peninsula. This school uses the Qiyas less than the two schools mentioned above.

4. The Hanbali (Haan-baal-ee) school was founded by Ahmed Ibn Mohammed Ibn Hanbal in Baghdad. Hanbal, who died in 885 A.D., established the most conservative school, which resisted all innovation, rejected the Qiyas and Ijma, and relied exclusively on the Koran and Sunna as the sources of the law. The Hanbali school predominates in most of Saudi Arabia today, although other schools have an influence in selected areas of the kingdom.

The evolution of Islamic or Sharia law halted in about 900 A.D., during the third century after Mohammed's death. Little change has taken place from that time. Since these rules are the word of God, man's only role is to administer them.

After World War I, the Arab world was essentially divided up between the British and the French. Both had an impact on Arab laws, the French imposing their civil law and the British their common law. However, the foundation remained Sharia law. After the Arab states achieved independence from the French and British following World War II, individual codes developed rapidly. In 1949, the Egyptians adopted their civil code, developed by Dr. Abdel Razak El-Sanhuri. This code represents a cross between Islamic law and the French civil code and has been exported to various Arab countries, including Kuwait, which approved its own version in 1961. Dr. Eugene Cotran, general editor of a new series on Middle East business law to be published by Graham and Trotman (London), has summarized the current status of contract laws in Arab countries:[1]

1. *Islamic or Sharia Law:* Saudi Arabia, N. Yemen
2. *Majalla or Ottoman civil codes:* Palestine, Jordan
3. *French-based codes:* Lebanon, Algeria, Tunisia, Morocco
4. *Egyptian-based codes—amalgam of (2) and (3):* Egypt, Syria, Iraq, Libya, Kuwait
5. *English/India influence but generally moving toward (4):* Sudan, Bahrain, Qatar, UAE, Oman, S. Yemen

This illustrates what one might have expected: there is a wide division in the progression of laws from state to state on the Peninsula. The extreme positions are Saudi Arabia and North Yemen in the more traditional role of law, and Kuwait and Bahrain at the other end represented by codified laws. However, it should be recognized that certain areas (such as family law and inheritance laws) are still influenced by the traditional rules of Sharia law.

Legal Systems on the Peninsula

Below is a country-by-country review of the legal systems on the Arabian Peninsula, beginning with the more traditional states.

Saudi Arabia

Sharia law in the kingdom covers criminal, civil, and international law. Since 1926, the conservative Hanbali school has been the official basis for all judicial decisions. This school recognizes only the Koran and Sunna as the source of laws and forms the basis for both the political and legal systems in the kingdom. In 1970, the Ministry of Justice was established to administer the judicial system.

North Yemen

Sharia law is in effect in this country, which generally follows the Shafii school. However, since North Yemen has a large population of Shia Mus-

---

[1]Eugene Cotran, "The Essentials of Contract Law in the Arab World," in *The Arab Business Yearbook*, London: Graham and Trotman, 1976, p. 363.

lims, the legal system is part Shafii rules and part Zaydi (*Zah*-ye-dee) law, the Shia rules of law. The significant difference with Shafii law is that it does permit Ijtihad (*Esh*-tee-haad), or personal reasoning by the judge versus the very strict interpretation by Sharia law. Thus there has been some flexibility in commercial and labor questions in the Sana courts.

Oman

The legal system in Oman is based on the Ibadi (Omani branch of Islam) interpretation of Sharia law. It stresses the Koran and Sunna as primary sources of law. Most cases are decided locally; and since Oman has a high illiteracy rate, oral statements by witnesses are given greater consideration than written evidence.

Decree by the Sultan comprises another type of legal rule in this country and recognizes areas not covered by Islamic law. Thus, in 1974 and 1975, decrees covering commercial firms, business guidance for private individuals and government officials, foreign trade and investment law, and a commercial code were issued. Also established at that time was an autonomous currency board.

United Arab Emirates

The UAE is a confederation of seven shaikhdoms formed in 1971. One of the activities not presently centralized is the administration of justice, which remains the responsibility of religious courts, called Qadi (Gha-dee) in each of the shaikhdoms. Under the 1971 constitution, an office of Attorney General was established; and the likely trend of the future will be a codified legal system for all legal matters in the confederation. The large shaikhdoms of Dubai and Abu Dhabi, which were protectorates of Britain until 1971, have been influenced by British common law. At present, each emirate has two courts: civil and Sharia (covering personal or family matters).

South Yemen

Up to 1967, South Yemen was a crown colony of the British. During that period, there were two court systems in effect. In and around Aden, the principal city, the British set up a network of lower courts which heard all civil and criminal cases. In the outlying areas, traditional Islamic law, called Urf or customary law, was the rule.

After Britain's departure, a series of courts was set up primarily to deal with former rulers and political prisoners. Not much remains of the British system, and the country has returned to the traditional rules of Sharia law. This is likely to be the case for some time.

Qatar

Prior to the adoption of a constitution in 1970, the ruler's authority often overlapped judicial activity, because he adjudicated disputes and grievances brought to him. This country's regular legal system is based on Sharia law and the very conservative Hanbali school, also recognized in Saudi Arabia.

In 1971, civil and criminal codes and procedures were introduced; and by the late 1970s, the courts were divided into secular courts covering criminal, civil, labor, and appeals, and religious courts primarily confined to family matters and issues of religious morality. Thus the last decade has witnessed an evolution that is more accommodating to commercial activity.

Kuwait

The Kuwaiti constitution, adopted in 1962, established the judiciary as an independent branch of government. Its legal codes, approved one year earlier, were the consolidation of several legal sources. Sharia of the Maliki school formed the basis, and the constitution did not permit laws to be in conflict with religious laws.

The new Kuwaiti codes incorporated much of Egyptian and Iraqi experiences, which were based on the French civil code, as well as the Bahraini experiences, which were influenced by British common law. Also having an influence on the new codes were the Majalla or Ottoman civil codes of 1876. Kuwait has one of the more progressive legal systems in the area, and on occasion foreign lawyers have been allowed to practice in the country.

Bahrain

Under the influence of British legal advisers, Bahrain was the first Gulf state to develop a non-Islamic legal system, beginning in the mid 1920s. In 1969, it adopted contract laws patterned after Indian contract law, also an outgrowth of British rule. Bahraini laws are still evolving and incorporate many sources: Urf or customary tribal laws, both the Maliki and the Shafii schools of Sunni Islamic law, Shia Sharia laws, and British common law.

The Amir of Bahrain is the first source of appeal from decisions of the courts. While Bahrain's legal system is as progressive as any on the Peninsula, it does maintain a dual court system of civil courts and Sharia courts.

It should be clear from this review of the legal systems of the Arabian Peninsula that there is a wide divergence between the more traditional and more progressive states. But each state, no matter how progressive its code systems may appear to be, has a legal system founded on Sharia law.

What does all this tell the eager Western businessman hoping to establish a new relationship in one of these countries? The obvious message, even if the businessman has a legal background, is that he will need local legal help to succeed in this new arena. A Western-trained lawyer does not have a chance. There is too much that is new, too much variance from one country to the next. Therefore, one of the first issues to address after arriving in one of the target countries is the selection of a local legal counsel. The local American and British embassies, local banks, and local chambers of commerce are good sources for the names of possible counsel.

5

The Importance of the In-Country Contact: Agent/Sponsor/ Representative/Partner

Few decisions made by a firm trying to penetrate a market in one of the target countries will have greater significance than proper selection of the in-country contact. These people are referred to by various titles: agent, sponsor, representative, partner. Whatever they are called, they can spell the difference between success or failure in a Middle East nation.

Half the countries on the Peninsula require the use of an agent by law. The requirement is by no means uniform, and the practices vary from state to state. Even in those areas that do not require an agent, it is likely that your project will fare better if your firm is represented by a local contact who can guide you through the maze of Arab culture.

Although the title of the local contact will vary, there are two fundamental types. The most common type—often called an agent, sponsor, or representative—will take a share of the profits (usually a percentage) but will have no say in the management of the enterprise. An agent works for you as any other employee would. The second and less common type—the local partner—will have a say in the management of the project. More important, he will be in an equity position through the life of the agreement or your operation in that country. Thus you will want to weigh carefully your choice of a local partner.

Your local contact, depending upon his background, can perform a number of valuable services which you would find difficult to do as a foreigner in this culture. Many are simply administrative in nature and may seem trivial—unless, of course, you've been stranded overnight in an airport terminal because someone forgot to obtain a visa for you. Visas, both entry and exit, are obvious duties for your local contact, as are hotel reservations, flight reservations, local transportation, and translation. Once your project is under way, you are likely to need work permits for some of your expatriate staff on local assignment. Just cutting through the local bureaucracy in such simple tasks as getting a package out of customs can be a nightmare for a foreigner. Your local representative, in his home environment, can outperform you in every instance.

Of more significance to you than these administrative functions is the marketing and management assistance your local representative can provide. He can, through his contacts, friends, and relatives, keep watch for new projects, awards, and tenders on the horizon. He can look for changes in the local laws that may affect your project. Often, he will be able to arrange for some type of financial assistance, depending on the nature of your endeavor. Once you receive a request for a local tender, the agent can provide valuable help in handling tender registration requirements—which in the Arab world often make U.S. government requests for proposals seem comicbook simple. Should you win the competition, your contact can help fulfill the labor and material requirements.

One of the most important functions of your agent will be the proper introduction to local government officials and businessmen. As an outsider, you will not know who is important to the success of your project. Finally, your agent can help you avoid the cultural pitfalls which can spell failure for even the most promising project. Of course, you will want to know something about the culture yourself, if for no other reason than to better understand the actions of your agent.

One businessman who has dealt with several Arab countries points out that the role of an agent in a more developed nation like Kuwait differs from that in other countries on the Peninsula. In most nations, he reports:

. . . you do not have proposals, bids, or tenders that will be publicly opened, with awards made to the lowest responsible bidder. Most proposals, bids, or tenders are *not* publicly opened, and the contract award is quite often more related to the "in" that your agent has with the contract giver than the nature of your bid, tender, or proposal.

Hence the importance of an agent, sponsor, representative, or partner is more related to his *connections—real not imagined*—than anything else. Once you reach the development and sophistication of Kuwait, the role of an agent changes.[1]

In Kuwait and probably Bahrain, an agent will perform in a more conventional role, and will be less able to use his influence to secure an award in your favor. As important as a good agent can be to the success of your undertaking, a bad agent can be a disaster, not only to the job being bid but to all future efforts in the country. As one authority puts it: ". . . mistakes are hard to undo, since terminating an agent resembles a divorce more than it does a simple management decision."[2] Even when your contract is specific, which is rare, and in your favor, local laws will protect the local representative over the foreigner. Even when your agent has done nothing for you except to collect his percentage, if the project is profitable you are certain to have difficulty terminating the agency relationship. Therefore, you must take great care in selecting your local representative.

Where can you get reliable recommendations as to a local agent? Probably one of the most dependable sources is your own embassy in the target country. Its commercial or economic officer (or attaché) will have a file on local businessmen and the projects and firms with which these businessmen have been associated. Often the attaché will know many of the people personally, and will certainly know them by reputation. Other embassies, particularly the British embassies, are frequently very helpful as well. Local branches of international banks are another source for recommendations.

In the United States, there are various organizations promoting U.S.-Arab business that may have some suggestions as to the selection of an agent. Branches of these organizations are located in New York, Washington, D.C., Houston, San Francisco, and Chicago. For details and addresses, see the selection on trade organizations in Chapter 2.

Finally, each of these countries has its own chamber of commerce to help you. This source must be used with care, however. Chamber of commerce officials are obviously influenced by pressures from local businessmen,

---

[1]Interview with Peter K. Simon, international business consultant in construction management, Leiden, Holland, November 4, 1979.

[2]Lillian Africano, *The Businessman's Guide to the Middle East*, New York: Harper & Row, 1977, p. 28.

friends, relatives, and so on. Suggestions from these officials should be examined closely for local bias. As one expert has stated:

> Checking and cross-checking of information with a wide variety of sources is advisable lest a businessman be led, as many have been, subtly or openly, into an unprofitable association with a friend or relative of one's initial contact.[3]

Some successful agents are overbooked, or may represent one of your competitors' products. Still others have made their fortunes and have gone into unofficial retirement. You do not need that kind of assistance.

One last cautionary word. When you have selected your agent, reduce your agreement to writing, and be as specific as possible about his duties. Include a provision for terminating the relationship under certain specified conditions.

Requirements for Using an Agent

Below is a country-by-country review of the requirements for using a local agent.

Bahrain

A local agent is not required by law, but in practice one is usually desirable. Wholly owned foreign companies are no longer allowed, but exceptions are made in the case of "offshore" chartered banks and commercial companies, which can operate regional branches.

Kuwait

By law, a Kuwaiti agent is required for all commercial transactions. An exception is made for consultants and engineers, as long as they are not offering management services. When they do, they also must have a local agent. All foreign firms with a local agent must be listed in the Commercial Register, maintained by the Ministry of Commerce and Industry.

[3]Dr. Nancy A. Shilling, "Commercial Regulations Applying in Arabian Peninsula Oil States," in *Middle East Annual Review—1978*, Essex, Eng.: The Middle East Review Co. Ltd., 1977, p. 44.

Oman

As of 1977, all foreign firms must use an Omani agent, who is registered with the Ministry of Commerce and Industry. Exceptions are allowed for consultants, engineers, accounting firms, and branches of international banks. Agreements for agents must be exclusive, but may be signed for a limited period of time. Local participation of not less than 35% is required on joint ventures, and participation of as high as 51% to 67% is required on other arrangements.

Qatar

By law, all foreign firms must use a local agent, and the agency agreement must be registered with the Ministry of Commerce and Industry. By special decree, exceptions are sometimes permitted. A joint venture must have 51% local ownership.

Saudi Arabia

In providing sales and services to the Ministry of Defense and Aviation, the use of an agent is prohibited by law. In all other commercial undertakings in the kingdom, a local agent is required. Preferential treatment in contract awards is given to firms with local participation at various levels:

> . . . although companies can obtain tax holidays for a space of five years provided there is a 25% local participation, there are attractions to the foreign investor to part with substantially more of the business than he normally might do. . . . Apart from the benefits of tax exemption, the surrender of 50% equity participation is considered by many entrepreneurs a small price to pay for the financial benefits that the company will reap by immediate large mobilization payments and long-term financing at cheap interest rates.[4]

One last point needs to be made with respect to the use of an agent in the kingdom. The person making the point asked not to be quoted by name—his business arrangements and contracts make the subject very sensitive.

> There are political alignments in Saudi Arabia, the liberal versus the conservative factions. If your agent gets you an audience with, say, Prince X,

[4]*Business Guide to Saudi Arabia,* Seven Arabian Markets Ltd., no city or date, pp. 38–39.

who is in one camp, and you attempt to then meet Prince Y, in the other camp, you don't stand a chance. A good agent will keep your identity from one side or the other until you win a program from one side. There are family divisions in the kingdom, and you want to avoid them and avoid agents who are aligned. The best source for locating a nonpolitical or non-aligned agent is the local banks, which can provide you with important contacts.[5]

United Arab Emirates

Since the UAE is a loose confederation of seven shaikhdoms, rules vary from one location to the next. Abu Dhabi requires an agent to do business. In other emirates, an agent is not required, but it is advisable to have one. While UAE law permits one agent for all the UAE, a local ruler may insist on the use of an agent from his shaikhdom. The trend is for a requirement of 51% local participation in all business projects.

North Yemen

An agent is not required by law. But because of the difficulty of doing business in North Yemen as a foreign firm, the use of an agent is highly recommended.

South Yemen

By law, not more than 50% of the profits may be removed from the country. This requirement has the effect of a 50% local participation rule. All foreign companies must deal through the Foreign Trade Company of South Yemen, a state-owned operation, which will act as agent for all trans-actions. The address is:

> The Foreign Trade Company
> Crater, Aden
> People's Democratic Republic of Yemen

Note: Every attempt has been made to provide accurate and up-to-date information on local agent rules. However, the use of agents on the Penin-sula is a fast-changing area. You should anticipate changes in the require-ments and make sure your information is current before you enter into an agreement. The U.S. Embassy will have the latest changes in the laws.

[5]Interview in Los Angeles, California, November 12, 1979.

6

Business Climate on the Peninsula

ALL the countries of the Arabian Peninsula encourage foreign participation in projects they feel are in their national interests. Some countries, such as the United Arab Emirates, actively seek foreign participation to aid their development plans. Others, such as Qatar, are more guarded in their solicitation of outside help; because of their substantial wealth, they do not feel a need to provide financial incentives to aid their development. The People's Democratic Republic of Yemen (South Yemen), a socialist state, prohibits foreign participation with local private sources. However, if the proposed endeavor is viewed to be in the country's best interests, foreign participation with the government as partner is possible.

Most of the countries have passed laws that specifically prohibit wholly owned foreign companies from operating in their territories. But exceptions are common when it is to the country's advantage to allow them. This is probably best typified by Bahrain's "offshore chartered bank" concept. By law, Bahrain requires 51% Bahraini participation when foreign firms operate on the island. However, when Beirut exploded into civil war in 1971 and foreign banks fled the city, Bahrain recognized an opportunity to capture the title of banking center of the Middle East. Bahrain's problem was how best to capture the relocating foreign banks without invalidating a law requiring 51% Bahraini ownership. The answer was simple: create a new category called "offshore charters" and award the charters on an exception basis to foreign corporations that operate on your soil. In 1977, the offshore concept was expanded to include commercial firms.

Kuwait and Qatar have similar 51% local ownership laws, but also allow for exceptions. Recently the UAE proposed a similar law, with Abu Dhabi and others approving it, but with some members taking strong exception, Umm Al Qaiwain in particular. Oman has a graduated system of local ownership: 66.6% for businesses that provide public information (newspapers, radio, television, motion pictures); 51% for businesses that provide public services (gas, electricity, water, transportation, real estate, aircraft, vessels); and 35% for all other firms. For a good proposal, however, exemptions are allowed.

The exact form of the business can vary considerably. Listed below are ten different types of organizations currently in use on the Peninsula, with the Arabic name shown in parentheses. Forms 1 through 6 are the most common; forms 7, 8, and 9 are primarily used in Saudi Arabia. Form 10, the sole proprietorship, is for information only, having little utility for the foreign company.

1. *Corporation / Joint Stock Company / Shareholding Company (Sharikat Mussahama)* is similar to the U.S. corporation. Shareholders subscribe to a specific number of transferable shares and are liable only to the extent of their investment.

2. *Joint Liability Partnership / General Partnership (Sharikat Tadhamun)* allows two or more people to form a partnership; the partners are jointly liable for the activity to the full extent of their personal assets.

3. *Limited Partnership / Mixed Liability Partnership (Sharikat Tawsiyah Baseetah)* allows two types of partners: general partners, who manage the activity and are jointly and severally liable for the operation to the full extent of their personal assets; and limited partners, whose liability is limited to the extent of their investment.

4. *Limited Liability Company or Partnership (Sharikat That Massouliyyah Mahdoodah)* permits two or more people to form a commercial activity, with each partner liable only to the extent of his capital share of the project.

5. *Partnership Limited by Shares (Sharikat Tawassiya Ashum)* allows both general and limited partners. As in form 3 above, capital is divided into shares, and the limited partners are subject to the provisions governing shareholders in a corporation (form 1 above).

6. *Joint Venture (Sharikat Mahassah)* is an unincorporated commercial agreement between two or more entities (individual or corporate) to accomplish a specific activity. A third person dealing with the joint venture has recourse only to the member with whom he deals—that is, other members do not have unlimited liability for one member's actions.

7. *Cooperative Company (Sharikat Taawoniyyah)* is normally formed for the purpose of improving the cost, purchase, or sales price of certain goods or services, and/or of improving the quality of same. It may be either a joint stock or limited liability company formed on a cooperative basis for the benefit of all members. Capital must be divided into registered shares of equal value, and all shareholders have equal rights in the company.

8. *Foreign Company (Sharikat Ajnabiyya)* is used in Saudi Arabia with the permission of the Ministry of Commerce and Industry. Foreign companies may obtain a license to set up branches, agencies, or offices to represent them. Such local representatives may issue securities for subscription or sale in the kingdom.

9. *Variable Capital Partnership (Sharikat That Ras-Al-Mal Al-Kabil Litaghayyar)* is a partnership whose bylaws provide for increasing or decreasing the partners' shares or for allowing admission of new partners.

10. *Sole Proprietorship (Mo-Assasah Fardiya)* is an enterprise owned by a single individual.

Government Incentives

The rulers on the Peninsula have been quite innovative in devising government incentives to induce new business into their countries. While there is not absolute uniformity from one state to the next, there is a pattern developing. Below is a rundown by country of the pattern as best it can be determined. This area is developing rapidly and may change at any time. Every attempt has been made to be accurate and to verify the information provided. One thing is clear, however: most of the states are receptive to a good proposal and will bend the rules or make an exception if the project is in their best interests.

Bahrain

There are no corporate taxes or personal income taxes in Bahrain. Profits and capital may be fully repatriated. New industries often receive customs and duties exemptions. The government will often provide assistance in obtaining labor, including the training of personnel, and will provide long-term low-cost land leases and inexpensive utilities for new industry.

Kuwait

Special privileges may be granted to new industries under the National Industries Law. These privileges take the form of exemptions from taxes and customs, low-interest government loans, free sites for industry, and tariff protection for the import product. Normally, there is a tax on corporate bodies but no personal income tax. All profits and dividends may be fully repatriated.

Oman

The only tax for foreign business is a progressive corporate tax ranging from 5% to 50%. However, if the project is in the "priority sector," the government will frequently allow a tax holiday for up to five years. Also, the government has been known to give low-cost long-term leases on land for new industry. There are no restrictions on the repatriation of profits.

Qatar

The government provides a series of incentives when a project is considered attractive and in concert with its development goals. There are normally no individual income or sales taxes, but firms are subject to a corporate tax. The Amir will often waive this tax for five years on projects he feels are important to his country.

On occasion the government will offer long-term low-interest loans, exemptions from customs and tariff protection, free leases with utilities at industrial sites, and government purchase of goods produced. Capital and profits may be fully repatriated.

Saudi Arabia

Since 1975, there have been no income taxes on expatriate salaries in the kingdom. There is a company profit tax; but often foreign firms have been able to negotiate an exemption to it.

The Zakat tax, an Islamic requirement at the rate of 1.25% on profits, is levied for the poor. In addition, Saudi social insurance is levied against both employer and employee at rates of 8% and 5% respectively. These two taxes are not normally waived by the kingdom.

Government incentives to induce new business include tax holidays, full repatriation of profits, free industrial sites, low-interest and no-interest loans, government purchase of locally produced goods, protective tariffs, assistance in site surveys, and help in recruiting and training personnel.

United Arab Emirates

There are no personal income taxes in the UAE. Both Abu Dhabi and Dubai have a tax on corporations; but thus far they have levied the tax only on oil-producing activities.

Each emirate in effect sets its own terms and conditions for new business; there are no UAE-wide regulations. In Sharjah, the ruler himself has taken an active role in obtaining new business and has appointed an American economist to help recruit new firms to the emirate.

Government incentives vary, but generally the shaikhdoms of the UAE have allowed tax holidays, long-term low-interest loans, rent-free sites, and other inducements. Profits are fully repatriated.

Yemen Arab Republic

By law, there is a tax both on expatriate individuals and on corporations; but thus far the government has not levied it on either and is not expected to change its policy in the near future. A five-year tax holiday is allowed for new firms. Companies are allowed to repatriate profits, but expatriate workers can send out only half the salaries they receive in-country.

The government has formed the Yemeni Company for Industrial Development to attract new firms. There is no requirement for local participation at present.

PDR of Yemen

One would not expect active solicitation of outside business in this new socialist country. Nevertheless, the government does offer certain types of incentives. Profits may be exempt from taxes for up to five years, provided the exemption does not exceed 10% of the capital invested. After deducting an income tax on salaries, expatriates may send out half their wages. Firms may repatriate half their profits. By law, South Yemen allows for mixed state and foreign ventures.

Chambers of Commerce on the Arabian Peninsula

Listed below are the addresses of the local chambers of commerce in the eight target countries.[1] In addition to the U.S. Embassy, the local chamber office should be one of your first in-country contacts.

Bahrain
Bahrain Chamber of Commerce and Industry
P.O. Box 248
Manama, Bahrain
Phone: 53749, 54702
Cable: TEJARA
Telex: 8691 TEJARA GJ

Kuwait
Kuwait Chamber of Commerce and Industry
P.O. Box 775
Kuwait City, Kuwait
Phone: 433864, 433865, 433866, 433854, 433855, 433856
Calbe: GURFTIGARA
Telex: 2198 GURFTIGARA KWT

Oman
Oman Chamber of Commerce and Industry
P.O. Box 4400
Muscat, Oman
Phone: 702259, 702319
Cable: ALGHURFA
Telex: 3389 ALGHURFAMB

Qatar
Qatar Chamber of Commerce
P.O. Box 402
Doha, Qatar
Phone: 23677
Cable: ELGHURFA

Saudi Arabia
Eastern Province Chamber of Commerce and Industry
P.O. Box 719
Dammam, Saudi Arabia
Telex: 601086 CHAMBER SJ

[1]*1979 Annual Directory,* New York: U.S.-Arab Chamber of Commerce, 1979, pp. 46–48.

Jeddah Chamber of Commerce and Industry
P.O. Box 1264
Jeddah, Saudi Arabia
Cable: THE CHAMBER
Telex: 401069 GHURFA SJ

Mecca Chamber of Commerce and Industry
P.O. Box 1086
Mecca, Saudi Arabia
Phone: 25775
Cable: CHAMBER MECCA
Telex: 440011 CHAMEC SJ

Medina Chamber of Commerce
P.O. Box 443
Medina, Saudi Arabia
Telex: 470009 ICCMED SJ

Riyadh Chamber of Commerce and Industry
P.O. Box 596
Riyadh, Saudi Arabia
Cable: CHAMCOM
Telex: 201054 TEJARYH SJ

United Arab Emirates
Abu Dhabi Chamber of Commerce and Industry
P.O. Box 662
Abu Dhabi, United Arab Emirates
Phone: 41880, 41881
Cable: TIJARA
Telex: 2449 TIJARA AH

Dubai Chamber of Commerce and Industry
P.O. Box 1457
Dubai, United Arab Emirates
Phone: 21191, 21327
Cable: TIJARA
Telex: 5997 TIJARA DB

Ras Al Khaimah Chamber of Commerce, Industry, and Agriculture
P.O. Box 87
Ras Al Khaimah, United Arab Emirates

Sharjah Chamber of Commerce and Industry
P.O. Box 580
Sharjah, United Arab Emirates

Phone: 22464, 351262, 351263
Cable: TIJARAH
Telex: 68205 TIJARA EM

Umm Al Qaiwain Chamber of Commerce and Industry
P.O. Box 436
Umm Al Qaiwain, United Arab Emirates
Phone: 69215
Cable: ALGHURFA
Telex: 9714

Ajman Chamber of Commerce and Industry
P.O. Box 662
Ajman, United Arab Emirates

No Chamber of Commerce is listed for Fujairah

People's Democratic Republic of Yemen
National Chamber of Commerce and Industry
P.O. Box 473
Crater, Aden
People's Democratic Republic of Yemen
Phone: 51104, 51203
Cable: GHURFATIGARIA

Yemen Arab Republic
Yemen Chamber of Commerce
P.O. Box 195
Sana, Yemen Arab Republic
Phone: 5917
Cable: CHAMBER SANA

7

The Economic Viability
of the Arabian Peninsula–
A Country-by-Country
Review

Back in 1974, Michael Field, a writer for the *London Financial Times*, completed a book with the dramatic title of *A Hundred Million Dollars a Day.*[1] In his book, Field talked about the tremendous amount of money flowing into the oil states on the Arabian Gulf in the 1970s. To illustrate the enormous purchasing power that $100 million represented, Field gave some examples of its impact in 1974. With this amount of money, you could have bought the Bank of America in 16 days, Exxon Corporation in 4 months, or IBM in just 7 months. Or you could have purchased all the industrial assets of Great Britain in less than 10 years.

In 1974, $100 million was indeed a tremendous amount of money. How-

---

[1] Michael Field, *A Hundred Million Dollars a Day,* London: Sidgwick and Jackson, 1975.

ever, if Field were to update his book today, only seven years later, he would have to double the value to $200 million a day—and there is no reason to expect this figure to remain stable for the next few years. OPEC, the international oil cartel,* has shown no signs of slowing the trend.

As noted in the introduction to this book, there has been a new world economic order since 1973. The pity is that too few people in the Western world fully comprehend the changed world marketplace. More than 50% of Americans recently surveyed were unaware that the United States imported any of its oil, let alone over half of it. Since 1973, most of the industrial nations of the West have reduced their per capita consumption of oil, but the United States has increased its per capita use of oil.

To properly place the new world economic order in perspective, we must first recognize that OPEC has, over protests from the West, increased the price of its commodity by over 1,000% since 1973—and the end does not appear to be in sight.

Second, we must examine the distribution of the world's oil reserves, particularly those concentrated on the Arabian Peninsula. As illustrated in Table 7–1, the Arabian Peninsula, with less than 1% of the population of the world, owns some 42% of the known world oil. Three states alone— Saudi Arabia, Kuwait, and the UAE—have 41% of the total. With this incredible level of new-found concentrated wealth, plus the fact that all the countries on the Peninsula are "underdeveloped" by Western standards, it can be seen that herein lie opportunities for Western businessmen. Opportunities are there, particularly for those businessmen who take the time to learn something about these new customers—in particular, to learn about their culture, as pointed out in Chapter 3.

Even those states that have little wealth in and of themselves, in the purely statistical sense, offer opportunities for a farsighted Western businessman by virtue of their proximity to these cash-surplus countries. As will be pointed out below, the North Yemenis have solved their trade deficit problem by shifting over a million of their workers into Saudi Arabia. These workers send home over a billion dollars each year.

To correctly assess the economic viability of the nations on the Arabian Peninsula, a country-by-country review is certainly required. This unique peninsula contains eight separate states, which include some of the very richest and the very poorest nations of the world, in both absolute (cash reserve) and per capita terms.

---

*OPEC is the Organization of Petroleum Exporting Countries. A cartel is defined as an international association formed to control the price and output of a given world commodity.

TABLE 7–1. A concentration of the world's oil wealth.

Country	Known Reserves			Population	
	Billions of barrels	% of World	Years of Production (at 1978 levels)	In millions	% of World
Saudi Arabia	165.70	26%	55	7.9	
Kuwait	66.20	10	97	1.2	
UAE: Abu Dhabi	30.00	5	57	.8	
Dubai	1.30		10		
Sharjah	.02		3		
Qatar	4.00	1	23	.2	
Oman	2.50		22	.8	
Bahrain	.28		12	.4	
North Yemen				5.1	
South Yemen				1.7	
Subtotal, Arabian Peninsula	270.00	42%		18.1	0.5%
United States	27.80	4	7	219.4	5.0
Mexico	16.00	2	33	65.5	2.0
USSR	71.00	11	17	261.2	6.0
All other nations	256.80	41		3,455.8	86.0
World	641.60	100%	28	4,020	100.0%

Source: Reserves and years of production (as of January 1979) from: Michael Field, "Oil in the Middle East and North Africa," in *The Middle East and North Africa 1979–80,* London: Europa Publications Ltd., 1979, p. 110. Population data from *1979 World Bank Atlas,* Washington, D.C.: World Bank, 1979.

The following section will address three issues relating to these states:

1. *Do they have the funds to pay?* There are underdeveloped nations across the world that desperately need new projects and ambitious development plans for carrying them out. Unfortunately, they often lack the funds to implement these projects. Can the nations of the Arabian Peninsula pay for new projects?

2. *Historically, what have they bought and from whom?* Over the years, what types of products have they imported and from which countries? Is there a buying pattern that must be overcome?

3. *What do they need and what are their potential growth areas?* Do they have a formal planning activity? Who does it and what does it call for? What are the best prospects for future sales?

In reviewing the material to follow, keep in mind that even in Western nations, including the United States, statistics are often inaccurate, distorted, and presented to support some position. Many authorities refuse to believe government data at all. If statistics are questionable in the West, how are we to view data from the Middle East, where precise recordkeeping has only recently begun? The answer is: carefully.

For example, it would be ideal if we could focus on the balance of payments for each nation over the years. But a balance-of-payments summary includes categories of funds, such as grants from nations, gold flows, trade balances, and even illegal activity such as illegal worker remittances to home and the smuggling of goods. Good records on much of this activity simply have not been kept—or, if kept, they are often not released. Therefore, we have to settle for something less than the ideal balance of payments.

Fairly reliable data have been kept on trade balances (the difference between what a nation buys from others and what it sells to others). Therefore, one of the tables that is displayed with some degree of confidence is a summary balance of trade for each country. In some cases the figures are given in local currency, with exchange rates at the bottom of the table.

Every attempt has been made to obtain reliable and up-to-date data. If the material is less than ideal, it is still the best uniformly available.

Bahrain

Bahrain has been a commercial trader for thousands of years. Since 1973 and the oil price increases, the nations around Bahrain have become the richest in the world. Bahrain is the "poor man on the block." Even though the first oil discovery on the Peninsula was made in Bahrain in 1932, the country's production level is down from a peak and quickly running out.

This small nation must return to its historical role as trader for the region. This it has done by picking up most of the banking business driven out of Beirut by its civil war. With its innovative offshore banking charter concept, Bahrain has allowed over 40 foreign banks to operate there without giving up 51% of the business to a local partner, as required by law. This is the largest concentration of banks in the area.

In December 1977, the offshore bank charter concept was expanded to include offshore commercial companies. This has allowed international companies desiring to set up a regional office to do so without having to give up 51% of the enterprise. Over 60 American firms have offices there. Thus Bahrain—with its easy-access 72-hour visas at the airport, excellent hotels with discotheques, fine food and liquor, excellent communication system, and innovative laws allowing commercial banks and regional offices to operate in the country—is truly becoming the Hong Kong of the Arabian Gulf. It's a pleasant place to visit and leave behind some recreational money.

Funds to Pay

A quick review of the trade balance position of Bahrain (Table 7–2), shows a nation with a problem: a trade deficit of considerable proportion.

What is not reflected in any published numbers is the amount of help being supplied to Bahrain by its wealthy neighbors Kuwait, the UAE, and Saudi Arabia. Considerable grants of funds are flowing from these countries to cover a number of health, education, and housing projects, although according to the Department of Commerce "the Embassy has no means of estimating the amount of direct assistance thus granted."[2] Even so, it is known that the School of Nursing was funded by a grant from Kuwait. The acute shortage of housing is being alleviated by funds from Saudi Arabia. The proposed causeway to the Saudi coast, a major construction job, is also being paid for by the Saudi kingdom. Thus it is probably safe to conclude that projects of benefit to the population of Bahrain and its charitable wealthy neighbors in the form of regional stability will continue to be funded.

Historical Customers

For over 160 years, Bahrain was a protectorate of Britain. The United Kingdom remains its largest trading partner today. But Britain is not as significant as one might expect. Bahrain buys goods from many sources.

[2]U.S. Department of Commerce, *Foreign Economic Trends: Bahrain, 78-038*, Washington, D.C.: GPO, April 1978, p. 8.

TABLE 7–2. BAHRAIN: Summary balance of trade (U.S. $ millions)

	1975	1976	1977	1978	Total 4 Years
Trade balance	5.0	(150.7)	(183.4)	(154.1)	(483.2)
Exports	1,205.1	1,520.6	1,849.8	1,908.9	6,484.4
(Imports)	(1,200.1)	(1,671.3)	(2033.2)	(2,063.0)	(6,967.6)

Source: U.S. Department of Commerce, *Foreign Economic Trends: Bahrain, 79–101*, Washington, D.C.: GPO, September 1979, p. 3.

TABLE 7–3. BAHRAIN: Major importing countries.

Country	Measures	1974	1975	1976	1977	1978
USA	BD (M)*	32	36	57	53	53
	% of Year	7%	8%	9%	7%	7%
	(% Change from 1974)		(+14%)	(+81%)	(+68%)	(+68%)
Australia	BD (M)	10	12	20	23	25
	% of Year	2%	3%	2%	3%	3%
	(% Change from 1974)		(+22%)	(+101%)	(+128%)	(+154%)
China, People's Republic	BD (M)	11	14	15	24	8
	% of Year	2%	3%	2%	3%	1%
	(% Change from 1974)		(+28%)	(+35%)	(+118%)	(−28%)
West Germany	BD (M)	8	11	25	26	37
	% of Year	2%	3%	4%	3%	5%
	(% Change from 1974)		(+39%)	(+200%)	(+217%)	(+345%)
Japan	BD (M)	23	27	54	69	65
	% of Year	5%	6%	8%	9%	8%
	(% Change from 1974)		(+18%)	(+132%)	(+197%)	(+187%)
United Kingdom	BD (M)	26	43	68	87	90
	% of Year	5%	9%	10%	11%	11%
	(% Change from 1974)		(+66%)	(+166%)	(+238%)	(+250%)
All Others	BD (M)	363	311	419	520	514
	% of Year	77%	68%	64%	64%	65%
	(% Change from 1974)		(−14%)	(+16%)	(+43%)	(+41%)
Total	BD (M)	473	458	660	802	792
	% of Year	100%	100%	100%	100%	100%
	(% Change from 1974)		(−3%)	(+39%)	(+70%)	(+67%)

*$1.00 = .3839 Bahrain dinars.

Source: *The Middle East and North Africa 1979–80*, London: Europa Publications, 1979, p. 252.

Table 7–3 lists the nations exporting products to Bahrain, the relative percentage position of each nation, and the percentage change, using 1974 as a base. While the United States has had an increase of absolute exports to Bahrain of from $32 to $53 million, its relative yearly portion of 7% per year has been constant. The increase over 1974 of 68% has only kept pace with the country as a whole, which increased its imports by 67% over the period. Thus the United States neither gained nor lost sales to Bahrain in the 1974–1978 period. Showing the best improvement relative to 1974 figures are West Germany and the United Kingdom.

Table 7–4 shows the types of commodities imported by Bahrain, expressed as a percentage of the total each year, with the total BD (Bahrain dinars) shown for the years 1975 to 1978 at the bottom. While the totals are increasing each year, there have been no major shifts in the types of commodities bought. Bahrain is a consistent buyer of machinery and manufactured goods.

Potential Growth Areas

Bahrain began its formal planning activity in 1967. It has just completed a five-year plan for the period 1975–1980, prepared by the Ministry of Development and Industry. Bahrain is one of the few nations on the Peninsula that will allow a businessman—or businesswoman—to enter the country and visit a government office without prior notice, without a previously issued visa, and without a local sponsor.

This is one country where the "unannounced" visit, so common in Western business, is likely to work. A business executive would have a good chance of obtaining the detail behind the new five-year plan (for 1981–1986) by simply flying into Bahrain and contacting the U.S. Embassy's economic office (phone 714151) and then contacting the Bahrain Ministry of Development and Industry (phone 53361) and requesting a meeting. In no other nation on the Peninsula is this approach recommended.

There is a demand in Bahrain for American products and services, but at increasingly competitive prices and delivery schedules. The competition is coming from the Far East, with Japan and Korea leading the way. The U.S. Embassy gives the best opportunities for American products:

> Construction of roads, electricity generation, Bahrain's first sewage program, and (beginning perhaps in 1979) the causeway between Bahrain and Saudi Arabia should keep this sector active, but less than in recent years.[3]

[3]*Ibid.*, p. 5.

TABLE 7–4. BAHRAIN: Types of commodity imports.

Category	1975	1976	1977	1978
Food and live animals	11%	10%	10%	11%
Beverages and tobacco	3	2	2	2
Inedible raw materials	1	2	2	2
Minerals, fuels, lubricants	2	2	2	2
Chemicals	8	6	7	9
Basic manufactured goods	24	25	24	22
Machinery and transportation equipment	37	40	36	38
Misc. manufactured articles	14	13	17	14
Total percent	100%	100%	100%	100%
Total BD (M)	233	388	445	453
(% change from 1975)		(+66%)	(+91%)	(+94%)

Source: *The Middle East and North Africa 1979–80,* London: Europa Publications, 1979, p. 252.

Additional opportunities include:

> Heavy machinery; chemicals; building materials and equipment; automobiles; foodstuffs; materials handling equipment; refrigeration and heating equipment; hotel, restaurant and hospital equipment; home and office furniture and furnishings; and leisure equipment.[4]

One of the premises of this book is that the best opportunities for new business in the 1980s will be in the countries surrounding Saudi Arabia. In the case of Bahrain this is not entirely true. Like Saudi Arabia, it is an overworked territory—the competition from the Far East is getting increasingly severe. Nevertheless, Bahrain does offer a new firm with little overseas or Middle East experience an excellent opportunity to attempt to penetrate a new marketplace.

Kuwait

According to a 1979 Department of Commerce publication, "Kuwait, with a relatively small population of 1.1 million, has one of the highest per capita income levels in the world ($15,480 in 1976)."[5] Population and income data on Kuwait vary (the World Bank, for example, reports another set of statistics). But even though the data may conflict, all point to the fact

[4]*Ibid.,* p. 14.

TABLE 7–5. KUWAIT: Summary balance of trade (U.S. $ millions).

	Fiscal 1975–1976	Fiscal 1976–1977	Fiscal 1977–1978*	Total 3 Years
Trade balance	6,525	4,891	5,851	17,267
Exports	9,859	9,718	10,482	30,059
(Imports)	(3,334)	(4,827)	(4,631)	(12,792)

*Estimates.

Source: U.S. Department of Commerce, *Foreign Economic Trends: Kuwait, 79–107*, Washington, D.C.: GPO, 1979, p. 2.

that Kuwait is one of the wealthiest nations in the world, with a per capita income of 50% higher than in the United States.

Over 70% of Kuwait's income is derived from the production of crude oil and natural gas. As in any country dependent on one product for the bulk of its income, local officials are frightened at the thought that this limited source of revenue will be depleted someday. Proposals to diversify Kuwait's industries beyond oil and gas are always welcome. All is not that bleak, however. Present known reserves are projected to last almost 100 years at 1978 production levels (see Table 7–1).

Funds to Pay

With 10 percent of the known world's oil reserves and a population of a little over 1 million, the government of Kuwait clearly has the funds to pay. Kuwait has the funds to pay for anything it wants. Over the past several years, the country has run a positive trade balance, as reflected in Table 7–5. Because Kuwait has taken in more money than it could spend, and has done so for years, it is one of the few nations in the world that has built up a large cash surplus. Substantial amounts of this surplus have gone to establish the Kuwait Fund for Arab Economic Development, which provides funds to friendly Arab states.

Historical Customers

For over 100 years, the British dominated the Gulf area on the Arab side. Yet that dominance did not seem to ensure Britain the major commer-

[5]U.S. Department of Commerce, *Marketing in Kuwait, OBR 79-18*, Washington, D.C.: GPO, 1979, p. 2.

cial role in the region. Kuwait is a good example. Table 7–6 shows the major importing countries of the period 1973–1976. In each of these years, Americans outsold the British in exports to Kuwait. The United States has maintained a consistent 14% of the total cash each year, and has increased its absolute dollar sales nicely since 1973 by +226%, compared with Kuwait's increased imports from 1973 forward of +209%.

But other countries have also done very well. Japan has increased its yearly share of the total from 18% in 1973 to over 21% in 1976. France too has done nicely, increasing its products by over 500% in the four-year period.

Those interested in a more complete breakdown of U.S. products going to Kuwait over the period 1975–1977 should obtain a copy of the Department of Commerce's *Marketing in Kuwait* booklet, published in 1979. This document lists 39 categories of products going to Kuwait.[6]

A listing of the types of commodities bought by Kuwait over the period 1973–1976 is shown in Table 7–7. Note that there was an important increase in the overall volume and in the category of machinery and transportation equipment, from 34% of the total to 42% over the period, or from 107 million to 407 million Kuwaiti dinars. That's quite an increase.

Potential Growth Areas

In 1978, a $250 million housing construction job went to a Pakistani firm in a very close competition—the second bidder's price was less than 1% higher than the winner's. Competition is getting severe.

Best prospects for U.S. exports to Kuwait will be:

> . . . in the export of technology and in design, construction, equipment supply, and management of the many public works and industrial projects to be undertaken. The Government is presently implementing a number of projects including housing construction ($4 billion), extension of motorways ($1 billion), expansion of electric generation and water desalination capacity ($1.2 billion), LPG plant ($1 billion), hospital construction ($200 million), marina/recreational facilities ($400 million), telecommunications and port expansion ($750 million), and tanker purchases ($300 million).[7]

Formal planning takes place in Kuwait by the Ministry of Planning. The country is presently into a five-year plan covering 1976–1981.

[6]*Ibid.*
[7]*Ibid.*, p. 3.

TABLE 7–6. KUWAIT: Major importing countries.

Country	Measures	1973	1974	1975	1976
USA	US (M)	147	219	430	480
	% of Year	14%	14%	18%	15%
	(% Change from 1973)		(+49%)	(+192%)	(+226%)
Japan	US (M)	186	265	387	689
	% of Year	18%	17%	16%	21%
	(% Change from 1973)		(+42%)	(+100%)	(+270%)
West Germany	US (M)	82	173	273	364
	% of Year	8%	11%	11%	11%
	(% Change from 1973)		(+110%)	(+233%)	(+344%)
United Kingdom	US (M)	107	127	244	252
	% of Year	10%	8%	10%	8%
	(% Change from 1973)		(+18%)	(+128%)	(+135%)
France	US (M)	28	61	79	169
	% of Year	3%	4%	3%	5%
	(% Change from 1973)		(+118%)	(+182%)	(+500%)
Italy	US (M)	44	62	108	147
	% of Year	4%	4%	5%	5%
	(% Change from 1973)		(+41%)	(+145%)	(+234%)
India	US (M)	27	44	53	129
	% of Year	3%	3%	2%	4%
	(% Change from 1973)		(+63%)	(+96%)	(+378%)
All Others	US (M)	422	605	814	1.001
	% of Year	40%	39%	35%	31%
	(% Change from 1973)		(+43%)	(+92%)	(+137%)
Total	US (M)	1,043	1,556	2,388	3,231
	% of Year	100%	100%	100%	100%
	(% Change from 1973)		(+49%)	(+190%)	(+209%)

Source: U.S. Department of Commerce, *Overseas Business Report: Marketing in Kuwait, OBR 79–81*, Washington, D.C.: GPO, 1979, p. 3.

While price competition is important, quality and timely deliveries will be just as important in the future. But one matter cannot be mentioned often enough in dealing with Kuwait and all the countries in this region: the importance of personal contacts.

Companies wishing to increase their share of the Kuwaiti marketplace must be prepared to visit this country often in order to maintain close personal relationships. Not to visit Kuwait often, and to rely fully on an agent, will cost the firm sales over the long run.

Oman

This ancient but newly emerging nation went through a boom-bust period in the 1970s and appears to be on a new boom period for the early 1980s. Oil, which accounts for 95% of Oman's income, hit a peak of 370,000 barrels per day in 1976 and started a decline to 350.000 then to 315.000 barrels in 1977 and 1978 respectively.

At that time, there were forecasts that oil production would be down to 200,000 barrels per day in the early 1980s.

However, through a combination of conservation measures and new oil-field discoveries, it appears that production will be back to 350,000 barrels per day by 1981. Thus, while Oman was a highly sought-after market up to 1977—a room in the capital city of Muscat wasn't available at any cost—efforts to capture this business declined by the end of the decade. The luxu-

TABLE 7–7. KUWAIT: Types of commodity imports.

Category	1973	1974	1975	1976
Food and live animals	17%	15%	15%	12%
Chemicals	4	4	4	3
Basic manufacturing goods	21	24	18	22
Machinery and transportation equipment	34	36	46	42
Misc. manufactured articles	17	15	13	14
Other	7	6	4	7
Total %	100%	100%	100%	100%
Total KD (M)*	311	464	693	972
(% change from 1973)		(+49%)	(+123%)	(+212%)

*$1.00 = .27235 Kuwait dinars.

Source: The Middle East and North Africa 1979–80, London: Europa Publications, 1979, p. 504.

rious 300-room Intercontinental Hotel, opened in November 1977, experienced high vacancies. The boom was over. But forecasts for the 1980s are optimistic again.

Funds to Pay

From 1976 to 1978, Oman had a favorable trade balance, as Table 7–8 illustrates. The government's annual budget ran a surplus in 1977 of $189 million, but the following year sank into a deficit of over $600 million.[8]

Oman's very rich neighbor, Saudi Arabia, has started to pay for selected capital projects that it feels will contribute to stability in the region.

> Saudi Arabia granted Oman $100 million to build a copper mining and smelting complex at Sohar which will also be fueled by natural gas. . . . Saudi Arabia will finance the paving of the Nizwa-Thurrait road.[9]

Thus, in assessing a given nation's ability to fund projects on the Peninsula, one must also look beyond the nation's borders (to Saudi Arabia, Kuwait, and the UAE) to determine if a pattern of support is developing.

Historical Customers

Britain continues to hold a substantial edge over all other suppliers to Oman, as Table 7–9 illustrates. The United States is tied for fourth position behind Britain, UAE, and Japan, and has increased its share nicely from 1976 to 1978 by 40%. The biggest gainer in this period was Japan, which increased its share some 70% over the two years.

The People's Democratic Republic of China has shown considerable interest in this market and plans to organize a trade fair in Muscat in the 1980s.

Potential Growth Areas

Spending on new projects will be tight in the 1980s and somewhat dependent on the amount needed for defense, which gets top priority over domestic projects. Oman has recently completed a five-year development plan covering the period 1976–1980, prepared by the Ministry of Development. Projects not on the new plan, which covers 1981–1985, will be difficult to implement.

[8]U.S. Department of Commerce, *Foreign Economic Trends: Oman, 79-044*, Washington, D.C.: GPO, 1979, p. 8.
[9]*Ibid.*, p. 1.

TABLE 7–8. OMAN: Summary balance of trade (U.S. $ millions).

	1976	1977	1978*	Total 3 Years
Trade balance	407.9	412.0	282.7	1,102.6
Exports	1,592.0	1,597.5	1,542.7	4,732.2
(Imports)	(1,184.1)	(1,185.5)	(1,260.0)	(3,629.6)

*Provisional.

Source: U.S. Department of Commerce, *Foreign Economic Trends: Oman, 79–044,* Washington, D.C.: GPO, 1979, p. 2.

TABLE 7–9. OMAN: Major importing countries.

Country	Measures	1976	1977	1978
USA	RO (M)*	15	22	21
	% of Year	6%	7%	6%
	(% Change from 1976)		(+42%)	(+40%)
West Germany	RO (M)	16	20	21
	% of Year	6%	6%	6%
	(% Change from 1976)		(+24%)	(+31%)
India	RO (M)	12	15	15
	% of Year	5%	5%	5%
	(% Change from 1976)		(+27%)	(+27%)
Japan	RO (M)	30	41	51
	% of Year	12%	14%	16%
	(% Change from 1976)		(+35%)	(+70%)
Netherlands	RO (M)	8	14	8
	% of Year	3%	5%	2%
	(% Change from 1976)		(+84%)	(0)
UAE	RO (M)	43	44	51
	% of Year	17%	15%	16%
	(% Change from 1976)		(+3%)	(+19%)
United Kingdom	RO (M)	48	70	68
	% of Year	19%	23%	21%
	(% Change from 1976)		(+46%)	(+42%)
All Others	RO (M)	80	78	92
	% of Year	32%	25%	28%
	(% Change from 1976)		(−3%)	(+16%)
Total	RO (M)	250	302	327
	% of Year	100%	100%	100%
	(% Change from 1976)		(+20%)	(+31%)

*$1.00 = .3456 Oman riyals.

Source: The Middle East and North Africa 1979–80, London: Europa Publications, 1979, p. 616.

Innovative proposals are always welcome in this part of the world. For example, a 100-room Holiday Inn, which has never been more than partially filled and is close to a lovely beach at Salalah in the southern part of the country, offers opportunities to a farsighted travel promoter. Thousands of Western expatriates fly to Europe from the Peninsula each year to spend huge sums of money. A charter tour to Salalah for R&R could well be highly profitable to the promoter of this package.

America's reputation for high quality and performance is well established in Oman. The many projects already completed offer opportunities for U.S. firms in the maintenance and operations business. Pan American World Airways maintains both the Salalah and Seeb airports for the government. Financial and contract management services appear to be needed.

> Favorable sales opportunities exist for air conditioners, telephone equipment, airport navigation and communications equipment, data processing equipment, foodstuffs, and to an increasing extent transportation and water processing equipment.[10]

Prospects for Oman appear bright as the country enters its "second financial coming" in the 1980s. But competition and performance requirements are getting severe: ". . . bankers in neighboring Dubai are already commenting that the new oil news means Oman's balance of payments should move into surplus in the 1980s, provided military spending is kept in check and political stability is maintained."[11]

Qatar

Qatar is the smallest state on the Peninsula in terms of population, with only about 200,000 local residents. However, with almost 1% of the world's known oil reserves, Qatar has one of the highest per capita incomes in the world.

Funds to Pay

Qatar is a cash-surplus nation; since 1974, it has taken in more money than it could spend, thus building up a cash reserve. Since 1973 Qatar has

---

[10]*Ibid.*, p. 9.
[11]John Whelan, "Dhofar Oil Strikes Raise Oman's Income Expectations," in *Middle East Economic Digest* (London), May 18, 1979, p. 7.

TABLE 7–10. QATAR: Summary balance of trade (U.S. $ millions).

	1973	1974	1975	1976	1977	1978	Total 6 years
Trade balance	420.0	1,698.0	1,333.0	1,418.0	885.2	1,128.8	6,883.0
Exports	614.0	1,965.0	1,783.0	2,183.0	2,139.0	2,348.3	11,032.3
(Imports)	(194.0)	(267.0)	(450.0)	(765.0)	(1,253.8)	(1,219.5)	(4,149.3)

Source: U.S. Department of Commerce, *Foreign Economic Trends: Qatar:* 1973–1974 data— #77–095, August 1977, p. 3; 1975–1978 data—#79–106, September 1979, p. 4.

maintained a positive trade balance, as Table 7–10 shows. This country has the funds to pay for projects of its choosing.

Historical Customers

Although Qatar has had a long-term trade relationship with the United Kingdom, Britain has been losing ground as the major supplier of products. The leading gainers have been the West Germans and the Japanese, whose increases from 1975 to 1978 were almost 500% and 300% respectively, as Table 7–11 indicates.

While the United States has not done well (or even maintained its relative position), as reviewed in Table 7–11, prospects for increased sales look good.

> The first U.S.-trained Qatari students have now returned to positions in the government and the local business community, and their presence is being felt. . . . As more students return, it is expected that the already visible trend toward utilization of American goods and services will become more pronounced.[12]

Competition for scholarships to American universities is severe, and even a few returned graduates can have a far-reaching impact on a nation with only 200,000 people.

Potential Growth Areas

While the Japanese have a solid corner on the automobile market, sales of other products and services appear to be wide open. Housing is scarce: a

[12]U.S. Department of Commerce, *Foreign Economic Trends: Qatar, 78-116,* Washington, D.C.: GPO, 1978, p. 6.

new three-bedroom villa may rent for as much as $50,000 per year. Planning is under way for a new university and a new international airport. Doha, the capital, still suffers from power blackouts during the summer months.

In a country that needs development and that has the funds to pay, there appear to be substantial opportunities for American businessmen who take the time to learn how to correctly pronounce the name of this small but commercially important nation of Qatar.

TABLE 7–11. QATAR: Major importing countries.

Country	Measures	1975	1976	1977	1978
USA	QR (M)*	201	258	464	461
	% of Year	13%	8%	10%	10%
	(% Change from 1975)		(+28%)	(+131%)	**(+129%)**
West Germany	QR (M)	151	252	344	851
	% of Year	9%	8%	7%	18%
	(% Change from 1975)		(+67%)	(+128%)	(+463%)
Japan	QR (M)	242	933	1,294	906
	% of Year	15%	28%	27%	20%
	(% Change from 1975)		(+285%)	(+435%)	(+274%)
United Kingdom	QR (M)	342	547	915	721
	% of Year	21%	17%	19%	16%
	(% Change from 1975)		(+60%)	(+167%)	(+111%)
All Others	QR (M)	674	1,310	1,833	1,651
	% of Year	42%	39%	37%	36%
	(% Change from 1975)		(+94%)	(+172%)	(+145%)
Total	QR (M)	1,610	3,300	4,850	4,590
	% of Year	100%	100%	100%	100%
	(% Change from 1975)		(+105%)	(+232%)	**(+185%)**

*$1.00 = 3.763 Qatar riyals.

Source: "Special Report on Qatar," *Middle East Economic Digest,* November 1979, p. 48, citing data from Qatar Department of Customs, Bureau of Imports and Exports.

Saudi Arabia

Since the mid-1970s, the Kingdom of Saudi Arabia has been the richest nation in the world, in terms of both its cash reserves in the bank and its oil reserves in the ground. It is generally accepted that the boom of the 1970s is over, and that the future will be characterized by greater competition and cost control. But with oil revenues hitting all-time highs in 1980 and much development still left in the nation, Saudi remains one of the more attractive marketplaces in the world today. Unfortunately, the world's business community is aware of this fact and competition is severe.

Funds to Pay

"With reserves and other assets sufficient to cover almost two years of government expenditures or three years of imports, the financial position of Saudi Arabia remains one of the strongest in the world!"[13] In 1977, a record spending year, Saudi Arabia spent 95% of its income. Stated another way, in the worst year since the boom started, the country's savings were down to a mere 5%. But from the United States' financial perspective, keeping only 5% of the nation's revenues per year seems very attractive. The Saudis have and will continue to have funds to pay for their own projects and for those of their friendly neighbors on the Peninsula for some time.

Table 7–12 shows Saudi Arabia's trade balance position for the three-year period ending 1979. (Figures for 1979 are estimates.)

Historical Customers

As Table 7–13 indicates, the United States has held a constant relative position, and as the base increases, the dollar has risen. But the outstanding gain from 1974 to 1977 was made by Italy, increasing its sales by more than 1,000%. Both West Germany and Britain also did well in Saudi Arabia during the period.

As Table 7–14 indicates, there has been a shift in the types of commodities imported by the kingdom. Over the period 1973–1977, food and live animal imports went down from 24% to 10% per year, while machinery and transportation equipment increased from 35% to 40%. The largest increase was in building materials, which was a result of the massive construction started in this period. Building materials increased its share from 7% to 22%

[13]U.S. Department of Commerce, *Foreign Economic Trends: Saudi Arabia, 79-057,* Washington, D.C.: GPO, 1979, p. 7.

TABLE 7–12. SAUDI ARABIA: Summary balance of trade (U.S. $ billions).

	1977	1978	1979	Total 3 Years
Trade balance	26.1	17.4	29.0	72.5
Exports	40.8	37.8	54.0	132.6
(Imports)	(14.7)	(20.4)	(25.0)	(60.1)

Source: U.S. Department of Commerce, *Foreign Economic Trends: Saudi Arabia, 79–150,* Washington, D.C.: GPO, January 1980, p. 2.

TABLE 7–13. SAUDI ARABIA: Major importing countries.

Country	Measures	1974	1975	1976	1977
USA	SR (M)*	1,735	2,538	5,739	9,621
	% of Year	17%	17%	19%	19%
	(% Change from 1974)		(+52%)	(+230%)	(+454%)
West Germany	SR (M)	612	1,017	2,538	4,320
	% of Year	6%	7%	8%	8%
	(% Change from 1974)		(+66%)	(+315)	(+605%)
Japan	SR (M)	1,616	2,267	3,731	5,981
	% of Year	16%	15%	12%	12%
	(% Change from 1974)		(+40%)	(+131%)	(+270%)
Italy	SR (M)	280	578	1,504	3,168
	% of Year	3%	4%	5%	6%
	(% Change from 1974)		(+106%)	(+437%)	(+1,031%)
United Kingdom	SR (M)	491	1,147	1,815	3,182
	% of Year	5%	8%	6%	6%
	(% Change from 1974)		(+133%)	(+270%)	(+548%)
All others	SR (M)	5,370	7,276	15,364	25,390
	% of Year	53%	49%	50%	49%
	(% Change from 1974)		(+35%)	(+186%)	(+372%)
Total	SR (M)	10,104	14,823	30,691	51,662
	% of Year	100%	100%	100%	100%
	(% Change from 1974)		(+47%)	(+203%)	(+411%)

*$1.00 = 3.40 Saudi riyals.
Source: *The Middle East and North Africa 1979–80,* London: Europa Publications, 1979, p. 648.

TABLE 7–14. SAUDI ARABIA: Types of commodity imports.

Category	1973	1974	1975	1976	1977
Food and live animals	24%	20%	16%	12%	10%
Textiles and clothing	10	9	9	7	7
Machinery, transport	35	36	40	43	40
Building materials	7	12	14	17	22
Chemicals	6	5	4	3	3
Miscellaneous	18	18	17	18	18
Total percent	100%	100%	100%	100%	100%
Total SR (M)	7197	10,149	14,823	30,691	51,662
(% change from 1973)		(+41%)	(+106%)	(+326%)	(+618%)

Source: *The Middle East and North Africa 1979–80,* London: Europa Publications, 1979, p. 648.

of a base that increased sixfold during the period after the oil price increase. Opportunities of this magnitude may never again present themself to the business community.

Potential Growth Areas

With its massive dose of new housing construction in the late 1970s, the kingdom's available housing has almost caught up with demand. Overall construction in general is not expected to reach the previous levels per year. And the U.S. share is in for real competition from firms in the Far East.

With many newly completed development projects and a limited indigenous workforce of skilled and unskilled labor, there would appear to be opportunities for firms offering maintenance and operations services:

> Perhaps the greatest opportunities for U.S. firms are in the service sector. Both the Saudi Government and private firms have acquired large quantities of sophisticated machinery and equipment during the past five years which will require maintenance services and, in many cases, operations contracts to ensure their useful functioning. Given the increased stress on manpower development, training contracts also present attractive opportunities. U.S. firms should also consider concentrating their marketing efforts on labor-saving products and technology in light of the expressed intention to limit the presence of foreign workers to the extent possible.[14]

The Saudis have just completed their second five-year development plan, which began July 9, 1975, and ended May 15, 1980 (note the Islamic cal-

[14]*Ibid.,* p. 8.

endar year). The minister of planning, Shaikh Hisham Naser, has announced general details of the third five-year plan. For the period covering 1980–1985, the kingdom anticipates expenditures of $250 billion, or roughly $41,000 for every man, woman, and child in the nation. In addition, it has set aside a reserve of $50 billion to cover possible inflation. The $300 billion allotted in the third plan compares with an estimated $202 billion spent in the second five-year plan.

Whereas the second plan emphasized infrastructure projects, the third plan stresses manpower development and development of production capability in the kingdom. Shaikh Naser stated:

> More than SR 68 billion has been allocated for the municipalities, more than SR 20 billion for housing, SR 37 billion for housing programs for the military sectors, nearly SR 53 billion for electricity, and as much for water and desalination projects.[15]

(Note: To convert Saudi riyals, SR, to dollars, simply multiply by .3. Thus SR 68 billion becomes roughly $20.4 billion.) This new plan is one of the best-read documents in the business world.

The kingdom still offers opportunities for sales, particularly for businessmen who are willing to give up part of the effort to a local joint-venture partner. "Most observers find that returns and competitiveness in Saudi Arabia are merely coming closer to sustainable international norms as opposed to the fabulous levels of the '74–'76 'oil boom' atmosphere."[16] Thus today Saudi Arabia would appear to offer only *great* opportunities for profits, as compared with the greatest opportunities in the recent past.

United Arab Emirates

The seven shaikhdoms of the UAE sometimes act as a single body. But in most instances, particularly in the business sector, they act as seven independent states. It is important that the prospective businessman understand this arrangement when attempting to penetrate the UAE market.

For business purposes, the seven states can be grouped into four types:

1. *Abu Dhabi:* population 270,000; wealthiest of the group with roughly 84% of the UAE's oil revenue; cash surpluses; has given up to 18% away in foreign aid.

2. *Dubai:* population 250,000; also wealthy but only a ten-year supply of oil remaining. Historical trader of the region; likely will compete with Bah-

[15]*Arab News* (Saudi Arabia), May 6, 1980, p. 1.
[16]U.S. Department of Commerce, *Foreign Economic Trends: Saudi Arabia, 79-057,* Washington, D.C.: GPO, 1979, p. 7.

TABLE 7–15. UNITED ARAB EMIRATES: Summary balance of trade (U.S. $ millions).

	1977	1978	1979	Total 3 Years
Trade balance	5,030	4,627	6,668	16,325
Exports	10,108	9,782	12,268	32,158
(Imports)	(5,078)	(5,155)	(5,600)	(15,833)

Source: U.S. Department of Commerce, *Foreign Economic Trends: United Arab Emirates, 79–085*, Washington, D.C.: GPO, 1979, p. 2.

rain as the services and commercial center of the lower Gulf; presently has the other 14% of UAE's oil income.

3. *Sharjah:* population 110,000; a minor oil producer, plus $20 million annual revenue; the ruler actively promotes business expansion.

4. *Ras Al Khaimah, Fujairah, Ajman,* and *Umm Al Qaiwain:* a combined population of only 130,000; dependent on funds from the national UAE budget or from Abu Dhabi.

As somewhat of a surprise to the rulers of the UAE, these shaikhdoms recently experienced a recession from their peak of 1974–1977. The small nation was clearly overbanked, with some "51 banks operating 316 branches, or one bank or branch for every 2,350 inhabitants."[17] Two banks actually failed during the period, and others are restricting loan activity.

Almost all of UAE's national income is from oil, which is down from its peak in 1977.

Funds to pay

With a population of under 1 million and 5% of the world's known oil reserves, the UAE clearly has the ability to fund projects. The problem is one of priority and timing. Since the OPEC price increases, the UAE has had a very positive trade balance position, as Table 7–15 illustrates. In the period 1975–1979, it ran over $26 billion in surplus trade dollars—not bad for a nation with roughly the population of Washington, D.C.

Historical Customers

The United States holds a third-place position in sales to the UAE, with Japan in first place and the United Kingdom in second. Table 7–16 shows

[17]U.S. Department of Commerce, *Foreign Economic Trends: United Arab Emirates, 78-105*, Washington, D.C.: GPO, 1978, p. 9.

the relative levels for the period 1974–1978. Note that during this period, the United States fell behind the overall UAE total increase; +142% versus +204%. There are clearly business opportunities in the UAE for American business firms. In the future, much competition is expected from West Germany, England, and other European countries that are actively seeking business in the Emirates.

TABLE 7–16. UNITED ARAB EMIRATES: Major importing countries.

Country	Measures	1974	1975	1976	1977	1978
USA	UAE D (M)*	580	973	1,257	1,337	1,404
	% of Year	9%	9%	10%	7%	7%
	(% Change from 1974)		(+68%)	(+116%)	(+130%)	(**+142%**)
West Germany	UAE D (M)	218	304	483	856	969
	% of Year	3%	3%	3%	5%	5%
	(% Change from 1974)		(+39%)	(+121%)	(+292%)	(+314%)
India	UAE D (M)	181	286	514	657	510
	% of Year	3%	3%	4%	4%	2%
	(% Change from 1974)		(+58%)	(+184%)	(+263%)	(+182%)
Japan	UAE D (M)	942	1,355	1,805	2,537	2,615
	% of Year	14%	13%	14%	14%	13%
	(% Change from 1974)		(+43%)	(+91%)	(+169%)	(+178%)
United Kingdom	UAE D (M)	577	1,073	1,540	2,110	2,386
	% of Year	8%	10%	12%	12%	12%
	(% Change from 1974)		(+85%)	(+166%)	(+266%)	(+313%)
All others	UAE D (M)	4,252	6,580	7,551	10,563	12,616
	% of Year	63%	62%	57%	58%	61%
	(% Change from 1974)		(+55%)	(+77%)	(+133%)	(+197%)
Total	UAE D (M)	6,750	10,571	13,150	18,060	20,500
	% of Year	100%	100%	100%	100%	100%
	(% Change from 1974)		(+57%)	(+95%)	(+168%)	(**+204%**)

*$1.00 = 3.84 UAE dirhams.
Source: The Middle East and North Africa 1979–80, London: Europa Publications, 1979, p. 815.

Potential Growth Areas

There is a major new development project at Ruwais, which is about 100 miles west of Abu Dhabi City, or roughly midway between Abu Dhabi and the Qatar peninsula. This project, which is expected to take some ten years and billions of dollars to complete, will result in a new city, port, and industrial complex. Gas presently is being flared at Ruwais, and part of the development will harness some 3 million tons of liquefied gas per year for exportation. Another part of the project is a new refinery.

Much attention is being given to the exploration of new oil and gas reserves. The French have actively moved into this area, usurping the United States' position.

With newly created cities being established out of desert sands, many with high-rise buildings and sophisticated equipment, there would appear to be opportunities for maintenance and operations services.

The recent recession experienced by the UAE has resulted in a climate of "business nationalism." In the future, joint ventures with bank partners are likely to receive preferential treatment over international firms wanting to hold on to 100% of their operations.

Yemen Arab Republic

North Yemen, as the YAR is frequently called, is the second most populous state, with about 30% of the population of the Peninsula. Along with Bahrain, North Yemen and the bordering South Yemen have the distinction of being the "poor kids on the block," with per capita incomes of less than 3% of their richer neighbors. North Yemen has no oil and few known mineral deposits of any value.

On the surface, North Yemen appears to offer the American businessman little sales prospects. But its strategic location next to some of the world's wealthiest nations, plus the various world powers almost tripping over themselves to offer it aid packages, makes this nation very attractive from a sales standpoint.

Funds to Pay

North Yemen has been running a trade deficit for a number of years. For the past eight years, it has imported more than 40 times what it has exported—a rather hopeless situation on the surface. But what a trade balance fails to record is over a million male workers crossing the border to work in Saudi Arabia. These workers have sent home over $1 billion in each of the last three years. Table 7–17 shows North Yemen's trade balance as well as the worker remittances for the period 1976–1979. The worker remittances have made the difference, and have put North Yemen into a positive balance-of-payments position for this period. Through a combination of circumstances, North Yemen is a financially viable nation, capable of funding a modest development program. Its rich neighbor to the north would likely give assistance to projects of benefit to the region.

Historical Customers

As can be seen in Table 7–18, which covers the selected years of 1973, 1975, and 1977, Japan has been the consistent major trader in North Yemen. Also important to North Yemen are West Germany, Australia, and Saudi Arabia. Of particular significance, however, is the improvement during the period made by the United States and India, both of which made impressive gains of +1,657% and +1,827% respectively with 1973 as the base year.

During the same selected period of 1973, 1975, 1977, there was a dramatic change in the types of commodities imported, as Table 7–19 shows. The importation of foodstuffs went down from 44% of the total to 28%; and during the same time, the importation of machinery and equipment went up from 14% to 31% of the total.

TABLE 7-17. YEMEN ARAB REPUBLIC: Summary balance of trade payments (U.S. $ millions).

	1976	1977	1978	1979*	Total 4 Years
Trade balance	(370)	(711)	(827)	(960)	(2,868)
Exports	12	19	7	5	43
Imports	(382)	(730)	(834)	(965)	(2,911)
Gross worker remittances	525	1,013	1,340	1,400	4,278
Balance of payments	245	279	340	350	1,214

*Estimate.
Source: Mideast Business Exchange (Los Angeles), August-September 1979, p. 26, citing data from Ministry of Finance, Central Bank of Yemen; and U.S. Department of Commerce.

TABLE 7–18. YEMEN ARAB REPUBLIC: Major importing countries.

Country	Measures	1973	1975	1977
USA	YR (M)*	5	22	84
	% of Year	1%	2%	3%
	(% Change from 72/73)		(+363%)	**(+1,657%)**
Saudi Arabia	YR (M)	30	57	374
	% of Year	7%	6%	12%
	(% Change from 72/73)		(+92%)	(+1,164%)
Japan	YR (M)	60	171	410
	% of Year	15%	17%	13%
	(% Change from 72/73)		(+185%)	(+583%)
India	YR (M)	9	27	178
	% of Year	2%	3%	6%
	(% Change from 72/73		(+192%)	(+1,827%)
United Kingdom	YR (M)	22	50	170
	% of Year	5%	5%	6%
	(% Change from 72/73)		(+125%)	(+670%)
West Germany	YR (M)	26	59	177
	% of Year	6%	6%	6%
	(% Change from 72/73)		(+132%)	(+592%)
Australia	YR (M)	27	44	160
	% of Year	7%	5%	5%
	(% Change from 72/73)		(+64%)	(+494%)
All others	YR (M)	232	551	1,479
	% of Year	57%	56%	49%
	(% Change from 72/73)		(+137%)	(+536%)
Total	YR (M)	411	981	3,032
	% of Year	100%	100%	100%
	(% Change from 72/73)		(+139%)	**(+638%)**

*$1.00 = 4.547 YAR riyals.
Source: *Yemen Arab Republic: Development of a Traditional Economy,* Washington, D.C.: World Bank, 1979, pp. 234–235.

Potential Growth Areas

North Yemen has the best potential for agricultural development on the Peninsula. All it needs is water moved into the right places. Therefore, one potential growth area is agricultural and water resource development. This is the type of project that Saudi Arabia might well underwrite as being in the best interests of the region.

TABLE 7–19. YEMEN ARAB REPUBLIC: Types of commodity imports.

Category	1973	1975	1977
Foodstuffs	44%	43%	28%
Tobacco and beverages	3	3	2
Manufactured consumer goods	15	16	14
Minerals, fuel, gas, lubricants	5	4	2
Chemicals	4	5	4
Rubber, wood, leather, paper	4	5	6
Construction materials	5	4	5
Machinery and equipment	14	15	31
Other	6	5	8
Total percent	100%	100%	100%
Total YR (M)	411	981	3,032
(% change from 1973)		(+139%)	(+638%)

Source: Yemen Arab Republic: Development of a Traditional Economy, Washington, D.C.: World Bank, 1979, pp. 230, 231, citing annual reports from the Central Bank of Yemen.

Major government projects call for the construction of one or more cement plants. A nationwide electrification program is badly needed, as well as road construction linking the ports with the interior and North Yemen with Saudi Arabia. A $100-million-plus job for construction of houses just went to the National Construction Company of Pakistan.

Developmental planning takes place under the direction of the Central Planning Organization (CPO). The five-year plan for 1977–1981 calls for expenditures by sector, as shown in Table 7–20.

Because of its remote location and lack of luxury hotels and other modern comforts, American business firms have largely left this market to the people from the Far East. Many American businessmen know only two foreign words: "Hilton" and "Intercontinental." If they can't get a response using these key words, they feel the market isn't worth pursuing.

But North Yemen has potential for businessmen who are willing to rough it slightly and who will work with the local people to develop projects of regional benefit. The country has a desire for American products—if only the price and promised delivery time are reasonably competitive.

People's Democratic Republic of Yemen

South Yemen, as the PDR Yemen is commonly called, is the only Marxist state on the Peninsula. After its political turn to the left in the 1960s, it be-

TABLE 7–20. YEMEN ARAB REPUBLIC: Five-year plan (fiscal years 1977–1981).

Category	YR (M)*	%
Agriculture	2,276	14%
Manufacturing	1,998	12
Electricity, water, and power	1,373	9
Construction	451	3
Mining	174	1
Transportation and communications	4,925	31
Housing	2,090	13
Public administration	1,963	12
Trade and banking	721	5
Total	15,971	100%

*$1.00 = 4.547 YAR riyals.

Source: *Yemen Arab Republic: Development of a Traditional Economy,* Washington, D.C.: World Bank, 1979, p. 150.

came isolated from its neighbors, which are all adamantly anticommunist. However, relations have begun to thaw and are gradually returning to normal. The most important neighbor, Saudi Arabia, recognized South Yemen in 1976.

Funds to Pay

South Yemen is an agricultural state, with two-thirds of its labor force involved in this activity. As a trader, it has bought ten times more than it has sold, as Table 7–21 illustrates. As with North Yemen, hidden factors make South Yemen's position fairly solid. The country has received large amounts of assistance from both Russia and Red China. It has also asked for help from Iraq and Kuwait; and Saudi Arabia has given hints of monetary support.

But perhaps of greater importance are the workers who go north to find jobs and send money home to their families. As Table 7–21 shows, by 1977 the amount of worker remittances had moved this nation into a positive trade position for the first time in several years.

Historical Customers

In recent years, the United States has not been a major trading partner with South Yemen. But as Table 7–22 shows, from a 0% share of the market in 1973, the United States captured some 4% of the imports to South

TABLE 7–21. PEOPLE'S DEMOCRATIC REPUBLIC OF YEMEN: Summary balance of trade (U.S. $ millions).

	1973	1974	1975	1976	1977	Total 5 Years
Trade balance	(106)	(166)	(157)	(241)	(295)	(965)
Exports	14	8	8	26	29	85
(Imports)	(120)	(174)	(165)	(267)	(324)	(1,050)
Worker remittances	33	41	56	115	180	425
Balance of payments	(4)	(35)	(24)	(18)	40	(41)

Source: People's Democratic Republic of Yemen: A Review of Economic and Social Development, Washington, D.C.: World Bank, 1979, p. 90.

TABLE 7–22. PEOPLE'S DEMOCRATIC REPUBLIC OF YEMEN: Major importing countries.

Country	Measures	1973	1975	1977
USA	YD (000)*	148	1,248	3,508
	% of year	0%	2%	4%
	(% change from 1973)		(+743%)	**(+2,270%)**
United Kingdom	YD (000)	4,332	8,649	11,985
	% of year	13%	17%	12%
	(% change from 1973)		(+99%)	(+177%)
Italy	YD (000)	547	1,229	9,010
	% of year	2%	2%	9%
	(% change from 1973)		(+125%)	(+1,547%)
Netherlands	YD (000)	1,825	3,049	6,350
	% of year	5%	6%	6%
	(% change from 1973)		(+67%)	(+248%)
Japan	YD (000)	3,319	4,707	21,166
	% of year	10%	9%	21%
	(% change from 1973)		(+42%)	(+538%)
USSR	YD (000)	549	3,419	6,023
	% of year	2%	7%	6%
	(% change from 1973)		(+523%)	(+997%)
All others	YD (000)	22,893	29,898	41,303
	% of year	68%	57%	42%
	(% change from 1973		(+31%)	(+80%)
Total	YD (000)	33,613	52,199	99,345
	% of year	100%	100%	100%
	(% change from 1973)		(+55%)	**(+195%)**

*$1.00 = .3415 PDR of Yemen dinars.
Source: People's Democratic Republic of Yemen: A Review of Economic and Social Development, Washington, D.C.: World Bank, 1979, p. 97.

Yemen by 1977—the best performance of any of the major traders for the period. However, Japan and Britain still hold the lead.

The types of commodities being imported are shown in Table 7–23. As with North Yemen, a major shift in purchases occurred during the period. Food and live animal purchases went down from 47% to 23% of the total, while machinery and transportation equipment increased from 8% to 35% of the total.

Potential Growth Areas

South Yemen recently completed a five-year plan for the period 1974–1979. The plan gave priority to improving fishing operations, which account for 36% of the nation's exports. Table 7–24 shows the planned expenditures as set in 1974 and the actual expenditures for the first three years of the plan. South Yemen missed its targets by substantial amounts. Geological research took a large jump. The UAE has helped South Yemen search for oil, which, if found, could mean a dramatic change for this nation.

The new five-year plan developed by the Ministry of Planning covers the period 1979–1983. In a state-controlled economy, much importance has to be given to the items specified in the development plans.

A review of the financial data on the two Yemens indicates that they have more in common than just their names. Both are poor; but because of out-

TABLE 7–23. PEOPLE'S DEMOCRATIC REPUBLIC OF YEMEN: Types of commodity imports.

Category	1973	1975	1977
Food and live animals	47%	35%	23%
Beverages and tobacco	3	2	1
Crude materials, inedible	4	3	2
Petroleum products	9	19	18
Animal and vegetable oils	1	1	1
Chemicals	4	4	3
Manufactured goods	17	17	13
Machinery and transportation equipment	8	17	35
Misc. manufactured articles	7	2	4
Total percent	100%	100%	100%
Total YD (M)	36	62	121
(% change from 1973)		(+72%)	(+236%)

Source: People's Democratic Republic of Yemen: A Review of Economic and Social Development, Washington, D.C.: World Bank, 1979, p. 46, citing PDRY Central Statistical Organization data.

TABLE 7–24. PEOPLE'S DEMOCRATIC REPUBLIC OF YEMEN: Five-year plan (fiscal years 1974–1979).

Category	Five-year Planned (as of March 1974) YD (M)	%	Actual (through 1977) YD (M)	%
Agriculture	27.7	37%	49.9	37%
Industry	13.4	18%	17.7	13%
Transportation and communications	19.2	25%	34.5	25%
Education	6.1	8%	6.8	5%
Social welfare and information	1.1	1%	7.8	6%
Health	3.4	5%	1.8	1%
Housing and municipalities	3.6	5%	8.3	6%
Geological research	.9	1%	9.1	7%
	75.4	100%	135.9	100%

Source: Planned expenditures: American University, *Area Handbook for the Yemens*, Washington, D.C.: GPO, 1977, p. 140, citing PDRY Central Planning Commission data. Actual expenditures: *People's Democratic Republic of Yemen: A Review of Economic and Social Development*, Washington, D.C.: World Bank, 1979, p. 105, citing Ministry of Planning data.

side aid and a labor force willing to go to the jobs, both have become economically stable. Both have shifted their foreign purchases, reducing the percentage imports of food and increasing imports of machinery and equipment.

The one major difference is that South Yemen is a Marxist state. Obviously, an entirely different marketing approach is required, even though its stage of development and required products and services are similar to those of North Yemen.

8

How the U.S. Government Hinders Your Overseas Sales

A FEW years back I lived in Tehran, Iran, where I was responsible for the American Peace Corps program in that country. The Peace Corps was there specifically at the request of the government of Iran. Under these circumstances, one would naturally expect that all agencies of the local government would support the program. Or would one?

In June 1974, 104 new Peace Corps volunteers arrived in Tehran for training. The ministry that was to issue residence permits for the volunteers refused to process such a "large" number of applications in less than one week. The local police threatened to fine the volunteers if they allowed their three-day visas to expire. The ministry that was to issue work permits for the volunteers declared that it would take weeks to process 104 applications. Yet the Ministry of Foreign Affairs, representing the government of Iran, had requested these volunteers.

Less than 90 days after I arrived in the country, I had to go into court to represent the volunteers. When the judge learned that there was an "American guest" in his courtroom, he immediately stopped the proceedings to serve tea to his foreign visitor. Compliments were exchanged, tea and cookies were consumed, and then the judge fined all 104 volunteers for allowing their visas to expire. Official invitations or not, no one seemed to be supporting the official policy of the host government.

That evening, I was in a state of confusion and frustration. Why would a government have a policy in one direction, and yet have all its organizations appear to be working in a counterdirection? Then the answer came crashing through to me: Iran was a "third-world country." Things like this happen in third-world countries, with their poor planning and disjointed bureaucracies. Things like this don't happen in the United States. Americans work together toward common goals in the best interests of their country.

Since 1976 the United States has been running trade deficits of unprecedented proportions. The U.S. dollar has taken a beating against most world currencies as a result of the imbalance of trade. Much dialog has come out of Washington on how best to cope with the problem. The official U.S. government policy would appear to support increased exports of American goods and services, in an attempt to lower the deficits. Americans work as a team to solve these kinds of problems.

However, since 1976, the U.S. Congress has passed, and the President has signed into law, certain acts that seem to run counter to the official U.S. policy of encouraging exports of American goods. So much for "third-world" theories.

As an American businessman attempting to do business in an overseas market, it is important that you understand these new laws. Failure to comply with this legislation could result in fines against your company of up to $1 million, fines against you personally of up to $10,000, and imprisonment of up to five years. Thus you should be aware of:

The Foreign Corrupt Practices Act of 1977.
The antiboycott laws and amendments of 1976 and 1977.
The Sherman Antitrust Act of 1890.
The Civil Rights Act of 1964.
The Foreign Earned Income Act of 1978.

The Foreign Corrupt Practices Act of 1977

The Foreign Corrupt Practices Act (FCPA) became law on December 19, 1977. It was the direct result of investigations by the Watergate special prosecutor and the Securities and Exchange Commission (SEC) into the use of company assets to influence foreign governments (sometimes called bribes). Certain payments to foreign officials which were questionable at the time are now defined as illegal by the act. (The complete act is reprinted at the end of the chapter.)

Although the act emphasizes illegal foreign payments, the word "foreign" in the title may be misleading. The act contains three main sections:

Accounting standards.
Foreign corrupt practices by issuers.
Foreign corrupt practices by domestic concerns.

The first section has nothing to do with foreign activity and is not necessarily related to corrupt practices. Thus the main impact of the act could well be on domestic firms that have no overseas business.

To further cloud the interpretation of the act, both the Department of Justice and the Securities and Exchange Commission are called on to enforce it. Justice's role is fairly specific, while the SEC sections are quite vague. Some observers feel that the SEC's enforcement of the accounting standards section could have a profound impact on business:

> It is only when one considers the probable applications and consequences of the new law in light of past SEC enforcement policies and practices that one begins to understand why certain commentators in the legal and accounting professions have viewed the act as the most significant expansion of the securities laws since their passage in the New Deal era.[1]

Since the second and third sections are identical except for the definitions of "issuers" and "domestic concerns," they will be discussed as one. An "issuer" is any company that has a class of securities registered pursuant to Section 12 of the Securities Exchange Act of 1934 or any company that is required to file reports under Section 15(b) of the 1934 act (or any officer, director, employee, or agent of an issuer or any stockholder thereof acting on behalf of the issuer). Any firm with stock listed with the SEC would thus be an "issuer" by definition.

To pull in the balance of the American business world, the act defines a "domestic concern" as:

> (A) any individual who is a citizen, national, or resident of the United States; or (B) any corporation, partnership, association, joint-stock com-

---

[1]Hurd Baruch, "The Foreign Corrupt Practices Act," *Harvard Business Review,* January–February 1979, p. 32.

pany, business trust, unincorporated organization, or sole proprietorship, which has its principal place of business in the United States, or which is organized under the laws of a State of the United States or a territory, possession, or commonwealth of the United States.[2]

The foreign corrupt practices portion of the act has five parts, affecting the conduct of "issuers" and "domestic concerns." These five activities, together, constitute a violation:

1. Use of the mails or interstate commerce
2. Corruptly to offer, pay, or promise to pay anything of value
3. To (a) any foreign official
    (b) any foreign political party, party official, or candidate
    (c) any person, with reason to know that said person will pass such values to (a) or (b) above
4. For the purpose of influencing any official act, or decision to not act, of (a) or (b) or (c) above
5. In order to assist in obtaining or retaining business.

It is likely that the courts will supply a liberal interpretation to activities falling within item 1 (use of mails or interstate commerce). One phone call eliminates this as a defense.

Issuers or domestic concerns convicted under the foreign practices section may receive fines of up to $1 million per violation. Individuals may receive fines of up to $10,000 and up to five years' imprisonment for willful violations.

The act excludes "facilitating" (grease-type) payments made to foreign persons whose duties are essentially ministerial or clerical. Thus a payment of, say, $100 to a clerk who refuses to process 104 residence permits in a three-day period would not violate the FCPA. Also excluded are foreign payments made in response to "extortion" or "threat of physical violence." In theory, the facilitating and extortion exclusions sound good. Using them as a defense may be a little more difficult. Companies should consider some type of documentation for such payments, perhaps even notifying the local American embassy.

The law is less specific about payments to the prohibited foreign officials made through foreign subsidiaries or agents. If a bribe is made solely by a foreign subsidiary, for the benefit solely of the subsidiary and not the parent company and without the knowledge or acquiescence of the parent, a vio-

[2]Foreign Corrupt Practices Act, Section 104(d)(1)

lation will be difficult to prove. But these gray areas will be difficult to defend as well.

The agent–company relationship, a delicate matter even before this act, is made more difficult by the FCPA. Lack of knowledge on the part of a company may not be a sufficient defense. The firm may be under an obligation to make inquiries as to the activities of its representatives. Also, large payments to representatives in excess of normal fees could be construed as a firm's constructive knowledge of shady activity. This may be fine in theory, but find an agent in the Middle East who will admit his fees are excessive.

Finally, there is the difficulty of the breakup. As *Fortune* magazine stated:

> An agent slated to be fired may retaliate by threatening to seek immunity and tell the prosecutor about the payoffs his corporate employer forced him to make—whether the corporation did so or not.[3]

As noted earlier, the other portion of the act, the accounting standards section, has nothing to do with foreign activity and is not necessarily related to corrupt practices. But it is likely to have the most significant long-term impact on American business. The section gives the SEC an expanded role in the everyday activities of all "issuer" companies, as defined earlier. It does not appear to apply to "domestic concerns," also defined above, in the present version.

The international accounting firm of Touche Ross has prepared an excellent write-up on the FCPA, with emphasis on the accounting provisions. The opening paragraph focuses on the heart of the matter:

> How a publicly held business is controlled and keeps its records are now matters of legal compulsion, with fines and jail sentences for offenders. These are probably the most significant facts of the Foreign Corrupt Practices Act of 1977 (the Act)—yet most of its publicity has dealt with the penalties for bribes of foreign officials.[4]

The act itself is very clear as to the accounting standards it expects. "Issuer" firms must:

> (A) make and keep books, records, and accounts, which, in reasonable detail, accurately and fairly reflect the transactions and dispositions of the assets of the issuer; and

---

[3]John S. Estey and David W. Marston, "Pitfalls (and Loopholes) in the Foreign Bribery Law," *Fortune*, October 9, 1978, p. 188.

[4]*The New Management Imperative—Compliance with the Accounting Requirements of the Foreign Corrupt Practices Act*, New York: Touche Ross & Co., 1978, p. 1.

(B) devise and maintain a system of internal accounting controls sufficient to provide reasonable assurances that—

(i) transactions are executed in accordance with management's general or specific authorization;

(ii) transactions are recorded as necessary (I) to permit preparation of financial statements in conformity with generally accepted accounting principles or any other criteria applicable to such statements, and (II) to maintain accountability for assets;

(iii) access to assets is permitted only in accordance with management's general or specific authorization; and

(iv) the recorded accountability for assets is compared with the existing assets at reasonable intervals and appropriate action is taken with respect to any differences.[5]

It would appear that the management of firms in the "issuer" class can no longer afford a passive role with respect to:

Organizations with clear lines of authority and responsibility.
Delegations of authority—documented.
Policies and procedures—documented.
Records and internal systems—documented.
Internal audits and controls which safeguard assets.
Independent audits by outside accounting firms.

Violations of the accounting provisions could result in fines of up to $10,000 for firms and fines of $10,000 plus five years' imprisonment for company officials, as provided for in the amended SEC act. Exceptions to the accounting provisions are made to firms acting in cooperation with the head of any federal department or agency responsible for matters concerning "national security."

No one can predict with certainty the full impact of the FCPA. Senator Lloyd Bentsen of Texas recently expressed concern that the act as presently written is a "massive handicap to American exports."[6] *Fortune* magazine probably reflected the feelings of many multinational executives when it wrote:

Why did so many presumably prudent, otherwise law-abiding businessmen spend hard-earned corporate cash on payments now labeled unnecessary

[5]Foreign Corrupt Practices Act, Section 102(2).
[6]Gerald R. Rosen, "Washington," *Dun's Review,* March 1980.

and repugnant? If it was because of a moral blindspot, the FCPA may be a cure. But if they paid because the economics of international competition demanded it, then the sinners will go right on sinning, while keeping a sharp eye out for all those policemen around the corner.[7]

Antiboycott Laws and Amendments of 1976 and 1977

There is nothing new about the Arab nations boycotting the state of Israel. For over 30 years the Arabs have attempted to put economic pressure on Israel and those who do business with that nation. What is new is the effectiveness of the Arabs' actions. While the boycott was mainly symbolic up to 1973, since that time the new-found wealth of the oil-producing Arab countries has put muscle into the boycotting actions.

There is also nothing new about the United States being opposed to the Arab boycott. Since 1965, when Congress amended the Export Control Act of 1949, it has been the official U.S. policy to oppose restrictive trade practices or boycotts by foreign nations to countries friendly to the United States. But the impact of the 1965 amendment was minimal at best, for it represented little more than an official statement of policy.

What is significant, however, is the recent series of laws that have been passed (or amended or rejuvenated) by Congress, the executive branch, and various state legislatures across the country—legislation that falls into a broad category called "antiboycott laws." These laws are every bit as significant as the Foreign Corrupt Practices Act in restricting those in or wishing to enter the American export business. As one lawyer from Illinois aptly put it in an address in 1977:

> This additional burden on doing business with the expanding economies of the Arab World has discouraged, if not precluded, a number of U.S. businesses, particularly smaller enterprises, from participating in the lucrative export business to the Arab World, further aggravating the U.S. trade deficit.[8]

Thus even the shop owner of a one-man operation who decides to start exporting his products to, say, Oman should have a general understanding of these laws and their requirements. Violations could mean fines of up to

---

[7]John S. Estey and David W. Marston, "Pitfalls (and Loopholes) in the Foreign Bribery Law," *Fortune*, October 9, 1978, p. 188.

[8]Andre M. Saltoun, "Regulation of Foreign Boycotts," *The Business Lawyer*, Vol. 33, No. 2 (January 1978), p. 568.

$1 million and jail sentences of up to five years. The U.S. exporter must understand the significance of:

The boycott provisions of the Tax Reform Act of 1976.
The 1977 amendment to the Export Administration Act of 1969.
The antiboycott laws of selected states.
The Sherman Antitrust Act of 1890.
The Civil Rights Act of 1964.

Arab boycotts focus on three areas: *primary boycotts,* or direct refusal by Arab nations to trade with Israel; *secondary boycotts,* or refusal to trade with firms that trade with Israel; and *tertiary boycotts,* or refusal to utilize, directly or indirectly, the products or services of firms that trade with Israel. American antiboycott laws focus on secondary and tertiary boycott activities by U.S. firms.

Members of the Arab League enforce their boycott activity by maintaining a "blacklist." A central office in Damascus, Syria, keeps the master list and performs the role of coordinator. However, there is a regional office in each member nation, and additions may be made to the blacklist by either the central office or any regional office. Without debasing the quality of the lists over the years, it is probably safe to say that many firms which probably should not be on the list have been added through the actions of low-level functionaries. Conversely, other firms probably should have been added, but because of their influence or the importance of their products they were left off the list. Hence, the maintenance of the blacklist has been something less than an exact science over the years. Life is full of inequities.

The first of the new laws to come along was the Tax Reform Act of 1976. It did not explicitly prohibit participation in the boycott; but if a firm did participate it would lose tax benefits on income resulting from such participation. In addition, Code Section 999 of the law imposed heavy reporting requirements on firms doing business with 21 Arab nations, including all the countries of the Arabian Peninsula: "Willful failure to file Form 5713 is punishable by a fine of up to $25,000 or imprisonment up to one year, or both."[9]

The U.S. Department of the Treasury has issued question-and-answer guidelines interpreting the boycott provisions of the Tax Reform Act of 1976. Copies of the latest guidelines are available from the Treasury Department (Washington, D.C. 20005).

[9]*Ibid.,* p. 567.

Perhaps *the* most important new law for firms doing business with Arab nations is the 1977 amendment to the Export Administration Act of 1969. The 1969 act was written to stand for ten years, but Congress felt the necessity to enact a major revision in 1977. The 1979 revision to the basic act essentially continued the provisions of the 1977 amendment, so this discussion will focus on the impact of the 1977 changes.

The 1977 amendment applies to actions:

> (i) Taken by "United States persons" (ii) with respect to activities in the interstate or foreign commerce of the United States (iii) with intent to comply with, further, or support any boycott against a third country friendly to the United States.[10]

In short, the act attempts to prevent discrimination against U.S. individuals or firms on the basis of race, religion, sex, or national origin. It attempts to influence the behavior of persons operating outside the United States and persons not residents of or even doing business in the United States.

Six activities are prohibited by the 1977 amendment, as listed below. In order for a violation of the act to occur, certain elements must be present in combination:

A U.S. individual
Taking one of the six actions listed below
In connection with U.S. commerce activity
With intent to comply with, or further, or support an unsanctioned boycott.

The six prohibited activities are:

1. Refusing to do business with another U.S. person for boycott reasons.
2. Refusing or requiring another to refuse an action based on discrimination because of race, religion, sex, or national origin.
3. Furnishing information about race, religion, sex, or national origin.
4. Furnishing information regarding past or contemplated business relationships with boycotted or blacklisted persons.
5. Furnishing information concerning charitable and fraternal organizations.

[10]*Ibid.*, p. 571, a quotation from the Export Administration Amendment of 1977, Pub. Law No. 95-92, Sect. 201(a), 91 Stat. 235.

6. Implementing a letter of credit containing prohibited conditions or requirements.

It is conceivable that a U.S. firm would be prohibited from simply answering a boycott questionnaire from an Arab buyer, and thus be precluded from competing for such business in total.

As stated earlier, U.S. antiboycott laws focus on secondary and tertiary boycott activity. They do not attempt to eliminate primary boycotts by a given nation. Therefore, six exceptions to the above prohibitions are allowed by the act:

1. Compliance with the importing requirements of a boycotting country.
2. Compliance with import and shipping documentation requirements.
3. Compliance with a unilateral and specific selection of carriers, insurers, or suppliers of services by the boycotting nation, performed within the borders of that nation.
4. Compliance with the exporting requirements of a boycotting country.
5. Compliance with immigration, passport, visa, or employment requirements of a boycotting country.
6. Compliance with local host country law.

Again, these exceptions apply only to primary boycott activity and will not give relief in secondary or tertiary boycotts.

Penalties for willful violations of the act are quite severe and constitute a criminal offense. A first violation may result in fines of up to $25,000 and/or one year in jail. A second violation may bring fines of up to $50,000 and jail sentences of up to five years. Additional civil penalties of up to $10,000 per violation may be assessed.

If the above two laws were not sufficient to completely shut down all trade with the Arab nations, certain states have gotten into the act. By 1977, eight states had passed antiboycott laws: California, Illinois, Maryland, Massachusetts, New York, Ohio, Minnesota, and New Jersey.[11]

In the long run, these state laws may have little effect because they appear to be in conflict with the 1977 amendment and, therefore, could be declared unconstitutional. However, until that time, they do pose a threat to firms in any of the above states. A small firm paying out thousands of dollars in legal fees to get a state law declared unconstitutional would find little comfort in a victory.

[11]*Ibid.*, p. 589.

One such antiboycott law is the "Berman Act" in California. It represents one of the more severe state laws. The act prohibits:

> —the exclusion of any person, natural or corporate, from any business transaction on the basis of a policy imposed by a third party (e.g., an Arab government) requiring discrimination on the basis of sex, race, color, religion, ancestry, national origin, or place of doing business (e.g., Israel).[12]

The act provides for fines to corporations of up to $1 million—yes, a million dollars—and personal fines of up to $100,000 and imprisonment of up to three years. Should there be any money left after the above fines, victims are able to obtain civil relief with up to treble damages.

The Sherman Antitrust Act of 1890

The Sherman Antitrust Act was passed on July 2, 1890, over 50 years before the state of Israel was created. However, participation in Arab boycott activity could be and has been considered to be in compliance with the "contract, combination, or conspiracy" sections of the Sherman Act and thus in violation of it.

The Civil Rights Act of 1964

Another federal law that could be violated as a result of boycott compliance is the Civil Rights Act of 1964, specifically Title VII. This act prohibits employment discrimination based on sex, religion, or national origin, among other considerations. Thus, if you receive an application for a Saudi assignment from a naturalized American woman from Israel, of the Jewish faith, you have a delicate situation on your hands. Good luck!

Foreign Earned Income Act of 1978

On one hot, sticky June night I awaited a midnight flight from Saudi Arabia to Pakistan. The old Dhahran terminal was never a pleasant place to visit, either coming or going. It was only a few years old, but its poor design entrapped the worst features of Middle East life: the heat, the smells, the humidity, the pushing and shoving of a frustrated populace.

[12]*Ibid.*, p. 590.

It was close to midnight, but the temperature was well over 100 degrees, with a humidity in the mid-90s. All the chairs were taken; most people were standing shoulder to shoulder. A few were lying on the floor next to the walls trying to sleep, oblivious to the noise and polluted air. Then an announcement came over the loudspeakers, first in Arabic then in English: the PIA flight to Karachi was ready for boarding. The terminal came immediately to life. There was excitement as the large group of Pakistani workers prepared to return to their homeland after months of working abroad. The armed Saudi airport guards showed irritation as this unruly mob pushed its way to the boarding gate. Exhausted, I boarded the tired 707 to Karachi along with 159 tired Pakistani workers, carrying 159 boxed Sony stereo radio cassettes.

The point of this story is those 159 Sony stereo radio cassettes. Some nations know how to give their people incentives to work toward national goals; other nations do not.

Pakistan does not enjoy a reputation for being a progressive nation. It is in a terrible financial position, caused not in small part by a chronic long-term trade deficit (somewhat like the United States'). But Pakistan is progressive enough to understand that trade deficits can be reduced or eliminated by the expansion of a nation's exports, either in goods or in services. The country does not have goods to export, but it does have a large, untapped workforce. Pakistan is thus an exporting nation of working people.

To encourage its people to go abroad, earn large salaries, and send money home, Pakistan offers a number of incentives. As in most nations of the world (the United States an exception), salaries earned abroad are not taxable at home. To further encourage its workers, Pakistan allows each laborer who has worked abroad for 12 months to bring home one tape recorder "duty free." Normally, to discourage imports from other nations, Pakistan places a 200% to 300% duty on all outside electronic equipment. A Pakistani laborer working 60-plus hours per week, earning about $300 per month, can thus earn the equivalent of, say, six weeks' wages by returning home with one $400 Sony stereo radio cassette, which he immediately sells on the black market. Pakistan may not be the most sophisticated nation in the world, but it does know how to use incentives to overcome national problems.

In the early 1970s an American living abroad, commonly referred to as an "expatriate," received considerable tax advantages. After he had met the necessary tests to qualify for foreign income exclusions, he could deduct the first $20,000 of his wages from his total taxable U.S. income. And under certain circumstances (three years overseas), he could receive up to $25,000 in exemptions from his income. Back in the early 1970s, $25,000 was a lot of money. It represented a tangible inducement to lease out one's home and go overseas for the attractive high salaries.

Today, a decade later, considerable changes have taken place. Most Americans are making much higher salaries than they were a decade ago, caused primarily by inflation at home and abroad. But instead of enacting legislation to keep pace with the higher salaries, Congress has passed a new law which reduces the attractiveness of overseas assignments. In November of 1978, President Carter signed into law the Foreign Earned Income Act. As an American planning to work overseas for some firm, or as a manager attempting to recruit people for overseas assignments with your firm, you should have a general understanding of the provisions of this act.

All citizens and resident aliens of the United States are subject to U.S. income tax laws, on income earned anywhere in the world. However, as an expatriate earning income from an overseas assignment, under certain qualifying conditions you will be entitled to a group of special exclusions from your gross income. The five categories are cost of living, home leave, costs of schooling, housing, and living in a "hardship" area. All countries on the Arabian Peninsula qualify as hardship areas, except for South Yemen, which does not appear on the approved 1978 list. The fact that the United States does not presently recognize South Yemen diplomatically probably accounts for the omission. Expatriates qualify after meeting one of two tests: they must be bona fide foreign residents or they must be physically out of the country for 510 days in a consecutive 18-month period.

The revised tax law is complicated, and no attempt will be made here to give the subject comprehensive treatment. Firms or individuals affected by the law should seek professional guidance. There are several international accounting firms qualified to give such assistance. Two such firms have produced excellent publications on the subject:

- [ ] Arthur Young & Company, *Taxation of U.S. Expatriates, 1978* (1979), 138 pages.
- [ ] Touche Ross & Company, *U.S. Taxpapers Living Abroad* (1979), 38 pages.

In short, even though salaries and the cost of living have perhaps doubled since the early 1970s, the tax benefits to American expatriates have, in absolute terms, stayed essentially constant. Since passage of the 1978 act, overseas exemptions have become so complicated that professional tax help is almost essential. But when the forms come back, ready for signature, one immediately finds that the total deductions under the new law are less than those under the earlier laws when present salaries and cost-of-living changes are taken into account. Here is a hypothetical case:

	Early 1970s	*Early 1980s*
Gross income	$50,000	$100,000
Expatriate exclusions/ deductions	(20,000)	(20,000)
Taxable income	$30,000	$ 80,000

It is obvious that the new law approved by Congress and the President reduces the incentives for doing business in the overseas marketplace.

If after reading the above sections, you have lost all urge to do business on the Arabian Peninsula, keep in mind that the worst is probably with us now. New legislation is likely to encourage rather than discourage the exportation of American goods and services.

A couple of years ago, while on the Arabian Peninsula, I observed a negotiation between two American firms. One of the negotiators had a favorite expression which seems to apply to the present legislative situation: "If you've got a man by the _____ (a delicate part of the anatomy), his heart and mind are sure to follow."

Today, the combination of a severe national recession and a continued severe trade deficit is certain to get the "hearts and minds" of politicians across the country. American businessmen cannot continue to compete against their British, German, French, Japanese, and Korean counterparts, who are not encumbered by such restrictions as the Foreign Corrupt Practices Act of 1977, the Foreign Earned Income Act of 1978, and the Sherman Antitrust Act of 1890. These laws are certain to be modified in favor of stimulating the exportation of American goods and services. At the very least, American workers are entitled to bring home one duty-free Sony stereo radio cassette.

TITLE I—FOREIGN CORRUPT PRACTICES

SHORT TITLE

Sec. 101. This title may be cited as the "Foreign Corrupt Practices Act of 1977."

ACCOUNTING STANDARDS

Sec. 102. Section 13(b) of the Securities Exchange Act of 1934 (15 U.S.C. 78q(b)) is amended by inserting "(1)" after "(b)" and by adding at the end thereof the following:

"(2) Every issuer which has a class of securities registered pursuant to section 12 of this title and every issuer which is required to file reports pursuant to section 15(d) of this title shall—

"(A) make and keep books, records, and accounts, which, in reasonable detail, accurately and fairly reflect the transactions and dispositions of the assets of the issuer; and

"(B) devise and maintain a system of internal accounting controls sufficient to provide reasonable assurances that—

"(i) transactions are executed in accordance with management's general or specific authorization;

"(ii) transactions are recorded as necessary (I) to permit preparation of financial statements in conformity with generally accepted accounting principles or any other criteria applicable to such statements, and (II) to maintain accountability for assets;

"(iii) access to assets is permitted only in accordance with management's general or specific authorization; and

"(iv) the recorded accountability for assets is compared with the existing assets at reasonable intervals and appropriate action is taken with respect to any differences.

"(3) (A) With respect to matters concerning the national security of the United States, no duty or liability under paragraph (2) of this subsection shall be imposed upon any person acting in cooperation with the head of any Federal department or agency responsible for such matters if such act in cooperation with such head of a department or agency was done upon the specific, written directive of the head of such department or agency pursuant to Presidential authority to issue such directives. Each directive issued under this paragraph shall set forth the specific facts and circumstances with respect to which the provisions of this paragraph are to be invoked. Each such directive shall, unless renewed in writing, expire one year after the date of issuance.

"(B) Each head of a Federal department or agency of the United States who issues a directive pursuant to this paragraph shall maintain a complete file of all such directives and shall, on October 1 of each year, transmit a summary of matters covered by such directives in force at any time during the previous year to the Permanent Select Committee on Intelligence of the House of Representatives and the Select Committee on Intelligence of the Senate."

FOREIGN CORRUPT PRACTICES BY ISSUERS

Sec. 103. (a) The Securities Exchange Act of 1934 is amended by inserting after section 30 the following new section:

"FOREIGN CORRUPT PRACTICES BY ISSUERS

"Sec. 30A. (a) It shall be unlawful for any issuer which has a class of securities registered pursuant to section 12 of this title or which is required to file reports under section 15(d) of this title, or for any officer, director, employee, or agent of such issuer or any stockholder thereof acting on behalf of such issuer, to make use of the mails or any means or instrumentality of interstate commerce corruptly in furtherance of an offer, payment, promise to pay, or authorization of the payment of any money, or offer, gift, promise to give, or authorization of the giving of anything of value to—

"(1) any foreign official for purposes of—

"(A) influencing any act or decision of such foreign official in his official capacity, including a decision to fail to perform his official functions; or

"(B) inducing such foreign official to use his influence with a foreign government or instrumentality thereof to affect or influence any act or decision of such government or instrumentality,

in order to assist such issuer in obtaining or retaining business for or with, or directing business to, any person;

"(2) any foreign political party or official thereof or any candidate for foreign political office for purposes of—

"(A) influencing any act or decision of such party, official, or candidate in its or his official capacity, including a decision to fail to perform its or his official functions; or

"(B) inducing such party, official, or candidate to use its or his influence with a foreign government or instrumentality thereof to affect or influence any act or decision of such government or instrumentality,

in order to assist such issuer in obtaining or retaining business for or with, or directing business to, any person; or

"(3) any person, while knowing or having reason to know that all or a portion of such money or thing of value will be offered, given, or promised, directly or indirectly, to any foreign official, to any foreign political party or official thereof, or to any candidate for foreign political office, for purposes of—

"(A) influencing any act or decision of such foreign official, political party, party official, or candidate in his or its official capacity, including a decision to fail to perform his or its official functions; or

"(B) inducing such foreign official, political party, party official, or candidate to use his or its influence with a foreign government or instrumentality thereof to affect or influence any act or decision of such government or instrumentality, in order to assist such issuer in obtaining or retaining business for or with, or directing business to, any person.

"(b) As used in this section, the term "foreign official" means any officer or employee of a foreign government or any department, agency, or instrumentality thereof, or any person acting in an official capacity for or on behalf of such government or department, agency, or instrumentality. Such term does not include any employee of a foreign government or any department, agency, or instrumentality thereof whose duties are essentially ministerial or clerical."

(b) (1) Section 32 (a) of the Securities Exchange Act of 1934 (15 U.S.C. 78ff(a)) is amended by inserting "(other than section 30A)" immediately after "title" the first place it appears.

(2) Section 32 of the Securities Exchange Act of 1934 (15 U.S.C. 78ff) is amended by adding at the end thereof the following new subsection:

"(c) (1) Any issuer which violates section 30A(a) of this title shall, upon conviction, be fined not more than $1,000,000.

"(2) Any officer or director of an issuer, or any stockholder acting on behalf of such issuer, who willfully violates section 30A(a) of this title shall, upon conviction, be fined not more than $10,000, or imprisoned not more than five years, or both.

"(3) Whenever an issuer is found to have violated section 30A(a) of this title, any employee or agent of such issuer who is a United States citizen, national, or resident or is otherwise subject to the jurisdiction of the United States (other than an officer, director, or stockholder of such issuer), and who willfully carried out the act or practice constituting such violation shall, upon conviction, be fined not more than $10,000, or imprisoned not more than five years, or both.

"(4) Whenever a fine is imposed under paragraph (2) or (3) of this subsection upon any officer, director, stockholder, employee, or agent of an issuer, such fine shall not be paid, directly or indirectly, by such issuer.".

FOREIGN CORRUPT PRACTICES BY DOMESTIC CONCERNS

Sec. 104. (a) It shall be unlawful for any domestic concern, other than an issuer which is subject to section 30A of the Securities Exchange Act of 1934, or any officer, director, employee, or agent of such domestic concern or any stockholder thereof acting on behalf of such domestic concern, to make use of the mails or any means or instrumentality of interstate commerce corruptly in furtherance of an offer, payment, promise to pay, or authorization of the payment of any money, or offer, gift, promise to give, or authorization of the giving of anything of value to—

(1) any foreign official for purposes of—

(A) influencing any act or decision of such foreign official in his official capacity, including a decision to fail to perform his official functions; or

(B) inducing such foreign official to use his influence with a foreign government or instrumentality thereof to affect or influence any act or decision of such government or instrumentality,

in order to assist such domestic concern in obtaining or retaining business for or with, or directing business to, any person;

(2) any foreign political party or official thereof or any candidate for foreign political office for purposes of—

(A) influencing any act or decision of such party, official, or candidate in its or his official capacity, including a decision to fail to perform its or his official functions; or

(B) inducing such party, official, or candidate to use its or his influence with a foreign government or instrumentality thereof to affect or influence any act or decision of such government or instrumentality,

in order to assist such domestic concern in obtaining or retaining business for or with, or directing business to, any person; or

(3) any person, while knowing or having reason to know that all or a portion of such money or thing of value will be offered, given, or promised, directly or indirectly, to any foreign official, to any foreign political party or official thereof, or to any candidate for foreign political office, for purposes of—

(A) influencing any act or decision of such foreign official, political party, party official, or candidate in his or its official capacity, including a decision to fail to perform his or its official functions; or

(B) inducing such foreign official, political party, party official, or candidate to use his or its influence with a foreign government or instrumentality thereof to affect or influence any act or decision of such government or instrumentality, in order to assist such domestic concern in obtaining or retaining business for or with, or directing business to, any person.

(b) (1) (A) Except as provided in subparagraph (B), any domestic concern which violates subsection (a) shall, upon conviction, be fined not more than $1,000,000.

(B) Any individual who is a domestic concern and who willfully violates subsection (a) shall, upon conviction, be fined not more than $10,000, or imprisoned not more than five years, or both.

(2) Any officer or director of a domestic concern, or stockholder acting on behalf of such domestic concern, who willfully violates subsection (a) shall, upon conviction, be fined not more than $10,000, or imprisoned not more than five years, or both.

(3) Whenever a domestic concern is found to have violated subsection (a) of this section, any employee or agent of such domestic concern who is a United States citizen, national, or resident or is otherwise subject to the jurisdiction of the United States (other than an officer, director, or stockholder acting on behalf of such domestic concern), and who willfully carried out the act or practice constituting such violation shall, upon conviction, be fined not more than $10,000, or imprisoned not more than five years, or both.

(4) Whenever a fine is imposed under paragraph (2) or (3) of this subsection upon any officer, director, stockholder, employee, or agent of a domestic concern, such fine shall not be paid, directly or indirectly, by such domestic concern.

(c) Whenever it appears to the Attorney General that any domestic concern, or officer, director, employee, agent, or stockholder thereof, is engaged, or is about to engage, in any act or practice constituting a violation of subsection (a) of this section, the Attorney General may, in his discretion, bring a civil action in an appropriate district court of the United States to enjoin such act or practice, and upon a proper showing a permanent or temporary injuction or a temporary restraining order shall be granted without bond.

(d) As used in this section:

(1) The term "domestic concern" means (A) any individual who is a citizen, national, or resident of the United States; or (B) any corporation, partnership, association, joint-stock company, business trust, unincorporated organization, or sole proprietorship, which has its principal place of business in the United States, or which is organized under the laws of a State of the United States or a territory, possession, or commonwealth of the United States.

(2) The term "foreign official" means any officer or employee of a foreign government or any department, agency, or instrumentality thereof, or any person acting in an official capacity for or on behalf of any such government or department, agency, or instrumentality. Such term does not include any employee of a foreign government or any department, agency, or instrumentality thereof whose duties are essentially ministerial or clerical.

(3) The term "interstate commerce" means trade, commerce, transportation, or communication among the several States, or between any foreign country and any State or between any State and any place or ship outside thereof. Such term includes the intrastate use of (A) a telephone or other interstate means of communication, or (B) any other interstate instrumentality.

9

How the U.S. Government Helps Your Overseas Sales

THE previous chapter examined how the U.S. government hinders your overseas sales—in opposition to its own best interests. This chapter will address the other side of the coin: how the U.S. government helps your overseas sales. Unfortunately, the chapter will be relatively short. There is not much material of substance to review.

In 1979 the Carter administration took two positive steps which should, in the next few years, improve the climate for U.S. overseas business activity. These two steps, Reorganization Plans Nos. 2 and 3, will draw attention to the problem (trade imbalances) and hopefully focus congressional attention on the obvious solution (more favorable foreign trade laws).

Reorganization Plan No. 2 became effective in July 1979 and is the less significant of the two plans from a business perspective. The plan created a new agency, the International Development Cooperation Administration (IDCA), which will coordinate the policies, programs, and budgets of the Agency for International Development (AID), the Institute for Scientific and Technological Cooperation, and the Overseas Private Investment Corporation (OPIC). Of particular interest to the business community are the activities of OPIC. The programs of OPIC are designed to benefit American firms wishing to do business overseas, and will be discussed in more detail below.

Perhaps the most important move to be made by the government to support American overseas business was Reorganization Plan No. 3, which went into effect in November 1979. This plan had a number of provisions, among them:

• Upgrading the White House Office of the Special Trade Representative to the Office of the U.S. Trade Representative, who becomes the chief policymaker on all U.S. trade matters. The U.S. Trade Representative will serve on the boards of the Export-Import Bank and the Overseas Private Investment Corporation, and will become a member of the National Advisory Council on International Monetary and Fiscal Policies.

• Transferring administrative responsibility for most trade programs to the Commerce Department; renaming that organization the Department of Trade and Commerce (the renaming has not yet taken place); and creating within that department an undersecretary for international trade, charged with aggressively expanding U.S. export opportunities.

• Transferring from Treasury to Commerce administrative responsibility for the countervailing duty and antidumping laws.

Thus the newly created U.S. Trade Representative and the Department of Commerce clearly have responsibility for putting the United States back into the international marketplace. The trade prospects for American businesses as a result of Reorganization Plan No. 3 seem optimistic indeed. But not everyone is impressed. As *Business Week* points out:

> President Carter—after proclaiming a national export promotion program in September, 1978, and promptly forgetting it—still is not convinced that the nation must launch a high-priority drive to reverse the disastrous decline of U.S. competitive power in world markets.
>
> A half-hearted reorganization of Washington's creaky trade bureaucracy this year, forced on a reluctant Administration by Congress, has deprived this export program of badly needed leadership by dividing between Commerce Secretary Philip M. Klutznack, the chief trade administrator, and U.S. Trade Representative Reubin O. D. Askew, chief international negotiator and White House advisor on trade policy. So feeble is Administration backing for the sales efforts of U.S. companies in global markets that many U.S. businessmen overseas are unaware that the U.S. even has an export policy.[1]

[1]"The New Export Policy Works Like the Old—Badly," *Business Week*, July 21, 1980, p. 88.

Now for a brief review of four government sources that can assist you in penetrating or expanding your activities on the Arabian Peninsula.

Department of Commerce

The activities of Commerce were mentioned in Chapter 2. Without question, this organization will be the single most important source of assistance to you from the U.S. government. It is in business specifically to help you in your activities. And under Reorganization Plan No. 3, it has the added muscle to give you support.

Back in 1975, while I was serving as director of the Peace Corps in Iran, I attended a weekly ritual called the Country Team Meeting. It was what might be called a bureaucratic staff meeting, where each U.S. agency in a given overseas mission meets to exchange current information. At exactly 9:00 A.M. each Wednesday in Tehran, some two dozen people would enter a suspended metal bubble (for security reasons) and await the U.S. ambassador's arrival. The ambassador would chair the meeting and give each agency representative an opportunity to speak. Seated in a clockwise position around the ambassador were the defense attaché, the senior military officer (a two-star general), the political attaché, the administrative attaché, an undisclosed agency representative, the agricultural attaché, the Peace Corps director, the United States Information Agency representative, and the economic and commercial attaché. Of importance to you as a businessman is the last person—the economic and commercial attaché—for even though you may never meet him directly, he can be of invaluable assistance to you.

In Tehran the U.S. Embassy's economic attaché or commercial attaché (interchangeable terms) had a large staff devoted to helping U.S. business interests. The staff monitored local laws for changes that could affect commercial trade with the U.S. The staff also reviewed and translated local publications for announcements of commercial interest. The office of the economic attaché maintained an extensive library of clippings and periodicals, which were made available on request. It supported and sometimes arranged trade fairs to allow U.S. businessmen to display their wares. Areas of special interest (such as civil aviation, science, and petroleum) were covered by assigning staff members full time to investigate that business area. It was an impressive show of help to American businesses.

By contrast, in the little island nation of Bahrain, the above activities were performed on a part-time basis by a commercial officer who, among other things, served as "acting ambassador" when the U.S. ambassador was out of the country.

The significance of all this is that in each country where the United States has an embassy, there are people devoted to isolating commercial opportunities and introducing American businessmen to them. This is true whether you are a vice president of a large multinational corporation or an individual businessman. Realistically, of course, the VP will have certain advantages over the Ma-and-Pa exporter.

Periodically, the business intelligence from each embassy is summarized and sent back to the Department of Commerce, to be released in the form of booklets called *Foreign Economic Trends and Their Implications for the United States* (see Chapter 2). The booklets are usually revised once a year, with data on the more active nations, such as Saudi Arabia, updated more frequently.

In addition, Commerce has specialists who will advise businesses in all aspects of exporting or overseas business activity. A visit to any of the 61 district offices of Commerce is likely to bring a wealth of opportunities.

Export-Import Bank of the United States (EXIM)

The Export-Import Bank of Washington was established on February 12, 1934, by executive order, to finance trade with the USSR. A second Export-Import Bank was established at the same time to support business with all other nations. In 1936 the two were merged by act of Congress. EXIM became an independent agency in 1945. Its purpose is to assist in the financing of U.S. exports through loans, loan guarantees, export insurance, and discount loans to commercial banks. Loans are made in dollars and must be repaid in dollars.

Two types of EXIM financing are available: project financing and supplier credit. Project financing accounts for the largest dollar volume, roughly 75% of the outstanding dollars. Under this activity such "turnkey" projects as electric power, manufacturing, petrochemical plants, mining, and construction are financed. Included in the same category are large equipment exports, such as locomotives, heavy capital equipment, and commercial jet aircraft (the last category alone accounts for almost half of EXIM's obligations). The second activity, supplier credit, represents a lesser dollar volume but a greater number of activities. In an average year, some 3,000 exporters will participate in supplier credit programs.

Over the years, EXIM has established a financing network with hundreds of U.S. and foreign financial institutions. A number of programs have evolved during this period:

• Bank guarantees were established in 1955, allowing for repayments to U.S. banks that extend credit to foreign buyers on behalf of U.S. exporters.

• Credit insurance was started in 1961. In conjunction with approximately 50 leading U.S. marine and casualty underwriters, EXIM created the Foreign Credit Insurance Association (FCIA). This organization insures short- and medium-term credits extended by American exporters to foreign buyers against commercial and political risks.

• Discount loans were issued in 1969 to provide a source of funds during periods of tight money, at fixed credit rates to foreign buyers.

• A cooperative financing facility was established in 1970 to set up a network of foreign banks to finance American exports to overseas customers.

• The Private Export Funding Corporation (PEFCO) was created in 1970 as a result of an agreement between EXIM and the Bankers' Association for Foreign Trade. This organization, which is owned by some 60 major U.S. banks and large exporters, finances capital equipment exports at fixed rates, but with an EXIM guarantee.

Under its charter, EXIM must meet certain requirements that put the U.S. exporter at a disadvantage in the world marketplace. For example, EXIM must act as an independent corporation, producing sufficient income from its investments to sustain itself. It must raise funds from the private sector, at market rates, and make loans and loan guarantees with sufficient margin to produce an income for itself. By contrast, many foreign competitor nations co-mix their export financing with aid grants, sustaining subsidies, and other financing to stimulate their own exports. As *Business Week* recently pointed out:

> EX-IM is handicapped in competition with Government-subsidized credit agencies of other countries because it must borrow funds at market rates, in accordance with statutory requirement that it be self-financing. . . . EX-IM not only finances a much smaller percentage of the nation's exports than do its competitors but also must charge interest rates that are 2% to 3% higher.[2]

Even with these restrictions, EXIM offers the American exporter an attractive assortment of financing approaches, including initial feasibility planning.

Only the highlights of EXIM'S programs have been discussed above. Interested exporters seeking a more complete description should contact:

[2]"A Fresh Treat to U.S. Exports," *Business Week,* May 26, 1980, p. 50.

EXIM Bank
811 Vermont Ave. NW
Washington, DC 20571
Telephone: (202) 566–2117
Small Business Hotline: (800) 424–5201

Overseas Private Investment Corporation (OPIC)

OPIC began its operations as a part of the Agency for International Development (AID). In 1971 it was spun out from AID and became a separate agency. Its purpose is to encourage long-term private American investment in some 90 less developed nations friendly to the United States by providing assistance in political risk insurance, financing, and investment counseling.

Under its legislative extension of 1978, giving it authority through September 1981, OPIC must:

- ☐ Give preferential consideration to investments in nations with a per capita GNP of $520 or less (in 1975 dollars).
- ☐ Restrict its assistance to certain categories of projects in those nations with a per capita GNP of over $1,000 (in 1975 dollars).
- ☐ Give preferential consideration to investment projects sponsored by smaller businesses, defined as those not in the *Fortune* 1,000 industrial categories.

In addition, OPIC is not allowed to support projects of a military nature. However, even with these restrictions, many small and medium-size firms may find OPIC's help valuable in implementing their new overseas endeavors. As with EXIM Bank, described above, OPIC will sometimes support the initial feasibility study on a project falling within its guidelines.

OPIC provides insurance service in specific countries against losses through:

- ☐ The inconvertibility of local currency earnings and return of capital.
- ☐ Expropriation and sometimes abrogation of contractual rights.
- ☐ War, revolution, and insurrection.

In each case the loss must be a complete one, and in the last case (war, revolution, insurrection) the intent must have been the complete overthrow of a local government. Coverage is normally for the life of a project loan, or contract, and for 12 to 20 years on equity. Coverage is limited to up to 90% of a loss (the remaining 10% must be absorbed by the private firm).

Financial assistance may be provided for pre-investment all-risk loan guarantees issued to private U.S. financial institutions, and loans from its direct investment fund. Most loans are made in dollars, but in certain instances they may be made in a local currency.

OPIC allows for the financing of joint ventures between local citizens and a U.S. firm when the U.S. firm maintains a meaningful share of the equity, normally not less than 25%. It also allows for limited ownership of the project by the local government, normally not more than 49% of the total equity. Management of the project must remain in private hands, and there must be a strong showing of U.S. financial interest in the activity. Loans generally range from $50,000 to $3 million. Loan guarantees may run up to $50 million. Current commercial rates apply to loan values.

Additional information on OPIC assistance may be obtained from:

> Overseas Private Investment Corporation
> 1129 20th Street NW
> Washington, DC 20527
> Telephone: (202) 632–1820, (800) 424–OPIC

Small Business Administration (SBA)

In the past, the SBA worked closely with the Department of Commerce in assisting small businesses with their export activities. Whether this role will continue in light of the Carter administration's efforts to organize all overseas trade activity in one organization (Commerce) is not clear. In the meantime, small businesses should not pass up the range of loans and services available from the SBA. There are close to 100 SBA offices in the United States. Addresses may be obtained from the telephone directory.

There are undoubtedly other federal programs hidden somewhere in the bureaucracy to assist firms desiring to do business overseas.

In summary, the year 1979 saw major changes in the federal structure to give assistance to American firms in their efforts to export U.S. products. These changes (Reorganization Plans Nos. 2 and 3) are likely to produce modifications in the export laws in the near future. In the meantime, American exporters will have to carry trade-restrictive burdens to a degree not found anywhere else in the world.

After all is said and done, however, there probably isn't one American exporter who would not exchange Reorganization Plans Nos. 2 and 3 for just one less antiboycott or corrupt practice provision, or for an attractive foreign income tax law.

10

Conclusions

In past chapters, many facts have been stated and many opinions have been expressed. In most cases only the highlights have been mentioned. In a few instances, the information may no longer be current, since this is a fast-changing part of the world.

A brief quote from a book published in 1962 illustrates just how fast this area is changing. The writer is referring to the United Arab Emirates, then called the Trucial Coast:

> In the Trucial Coast there exists hardly any kind of administration. The population of the seven Sheikhdoms is estimated at 100,000, composed mostly of Bedouin tribes living at a bare subsistence level. The only town along the 400-mile coast is Dubai, whose inhabitants account for about one-fourth of the Trucial Coast's total population.[1]

The writer Ian Fleming, of James Bond fame, described Bahrain two years later as follows:

[1]H. B. Sharabi, *Government and Politics of the Middle East in the Twentieth Century*, Princeton, N.J.: D. Van Nostrand Co., 1962, p. 260.

> Bahrain is, without question, the scruffiest international airport in the world. The washing facilities would not be tolerated in a prison, and the slow fans of the ceilings of the bedraggled hutments hardly stirred the flies.[2]

Not long ago I had the pleasure of using the "washing facilities" in the modern, air-conditioned airport in Bahrain, and I can testify that Ian Fleming's description no longer applies; nor does the earlier description of the Trucial Coast. Abu Dhabi is a modern, well-planned city with high-rise buildings that give the impression of Long Beach, California. One decade in this part of the world can and does bring substantial changes.

Throughout this book much emphasis has been placed on developing an understanding of the Arab culture. In a part of the world where business dealings are on a highly personal basis, such an understanding is as important to a businessman as is a knowledge of accounting. In fact, it is likely to be of greater importance, for a lack of accounting knowledge is not apt to cost you a business deal. But cultural insensitivity or rudeness will. I hope that you will continue to expand your knowledge of these fascinating and warm people.

Below is a summary of the fifty most important points covered in this book:

1. This book is designed to assist the American businessman in understanding, appreciating, and penetrating the markets on the Arabian Peninsula today.

2. The Peninsula contains eight separate nations, each unique.

3. These eight nations have certain common threads (language, religion, and culture), but it is a mistake to view them as one.

4. The eight nations represent the very richest and poorest nations in the world today. But even the poorest are quite well off as a result of financial help from their rich neighbors.

5. In the 1980s, the best *new* business prospects on the Peninsula will not be in Saudi Arabia, but rather in the small nations just beyond the borders of Saudi Arabia. Unless established, the kingdom is a tough marketplace.

6. To best capture these new markets, American businessmen should know something about and have a genuine respect for the Arab culture.

7. There is a tremendous amount of material available on these eight nations, most of it obtainable by mail.

8. There are American-Arab trade associations in five cities in the United States, each providing valuable assistance to businessmen.

[2]Ian Fleming, *Thrilling Cities*, New York: Signet Books, 1964, p. 15.

9. The U.S. embassies in the eight target nations are valuable sources of business information. Each has a commercial officer or attaché.

10. Each of these nations has a local chamber of commerce, which is also a valuable source of information.

11. As more Arab businessmen attend Western universities, they will become more sophisticated buyers and will no longer tolerate cultural ignorance as they have in the past.

12. Arab names have a definite meaning and a sequence that is different from Western names; it is important to know the differences.

13. The Islamic religion has an influence over all aspects of life on the Peninsula, social, legal, commercial, and political.

14. The Islamic religion has five pillars. You should know what they are.

15. The Islamic calendar is different from the Western calendar. The year is 354 days long. In 1981 Muslims celebrated the year 1402.

16. Translations from Arabic to English are approximate at best.

17. It is important to get certain pronunciations correct, especially people's names and place names.

18. Women and commerce on the Peninsula do not mix. Bahrain and possibly Kuwait are exceptions.

19. It is best to avoid the subject of women when you are doing business on the Peninsula.

20. Israel is another subject that should be circumvented.

21. Pride, or face, is important to an Arab. In negotiations, always be prepared to give up something—in other words, never win everything.

22. In friendly relations with an Arab, expect physical closeness and do not be repulsed by it. It is a sign of friendship.

23. As a Westerner, you will be perceived as a stereotype, just as you will stereotype your Arab host.

24. You must learn how to do business on Arab terms, not on Western terms. If you don't, there is a Japanese businessman behind you who will.

25. There are certain dos and don'ts in the Arab culture which may seem minor to you but which are important to your customer. You should know them.

26. Arab culture is a vast subject. You should continue to expand your knowledge of it by reading and observing.

27. Islamic or Sharia law has four basic sources and is divided into four separate schools.

28. While Islamic law provides a foundation for all legal systems on the Peninsula, each country is unique in its application of the law. Islamic law is so completely different from Western law that a local attorney is required.

29. The selection of a good local attorney is a key decision for you.

30. An even more important decision, with lasting impact, is the selection of a local representative—the specific individual and the type of arrangement with him.

31. Half the countries on the Peninsula require the use of a local representative by law, and the requirements vary from country to country.

32. In disputes with your local agent, local rulings are likely to go against you, even if you are right. Nevertheless, put your agent agreements in writing.

33. Because of the various advantages (financial and source selection) of using a local partner, you should give this arrangement consideration in settting up your project.

34. Each of the eight nations provides various government incentives to encourage foreign business activity. In the case of the UAE, each shaikhdom offers a different assortment of incentives.

35. Even when a specific law is passed outlawing or restricting certain types of business activity, a given ruler is often receptive to a good proposal. The states are quite flexible if a proposal is in their best interests.

36. There are six or more types of business arrangements in use on the Peninsula.

37. General statements about business do not apply to all eight nations. Each must be examined individually on a specific matter. The U.S. Embassy in each location will stay close to the subject.

38. The Arabian Peninsula has the greatest concentration of wealth in the world today.

39. There are opportunities for business arrangements in all nations on the Peninsula, even the poorer states.

40. As an exporter, or someone doing business overseas, you should be familiar with three recent laws: the Foreign Corrupt Practices Act of 1977, federal and state antiboycott laws, and the Foreign Earned Income Act of 1978. Violations of these laws could result in severe fines or even imprisonment.

41. During 1979, the executive branch was reorganized to assist you in your exports or overseas business. You should know something about Reorganization Plans Nos. 2 and 3.

42. The federal government has several programs to assist you in your overseas business. You should know something about the programs of the Department of Commerce, the Export-Import Bank; the Overseas Private Investment Corporation; and the Small Business Administration.

43. Because Bahrain is an easy place to visit and has all the luxury and conveniences of the West, it is an overworked territory. Nevertheless, for a firm completely without experience in the Middle East, it may be a good place to start.

44. Kuwait, because of its relative long-term wealth and cash surpluses, is an attractive customer. The disadvantages are severe competition and the level of sophistication of Kuwaiti buyers, more and more of whom are being trained in the West.

45. Oman is about to enter a second boom period, and there are real business opportunities in this nation.

46. Qatar is a cash-surplus nation with good opportunities for sales; but for some reason it has been largely overlooked by Western firms.

47. Saudi Arabia still possesses the greatest wealth and the greatest concentration of new business opportunities on the Peninsula. Unfortunately, the competition is becoming quite severe.

48. The UAE must be considered seven separate markets. One shaikhdom, Abu Dhabi, has the funds to pay for sound projects in any of these markets.

49. North Yemen is a difficult place to visit and gives the appearance of being poor; but with financial help from Saudi Arabia, it offers excellent opportunities for new markets to Western business firms.

50. South Yemen, a Marxist state, offers some opportunities for Western firms with the government as a partner in ventures.

The Arabian Peninsula contains eight separate marketplaces—or, if one counts each shaikhdom in the UAE, there are fourteen marketplaces. These entities have the funds (their own or grant funds) to pay for products, and the desire for American goods. Much of their money was once our money. It's an exciting part of the world. The prospects for sales are virtually unlimited. Best of luck in your ability to penetrate these markets.

APPENDIX A

American Banks on the Arabian Peninsula*

Below is a list of American banks and affiliates in the target countries. In the event that there is no American bank in a country, a British bank is listed. In two cases (Kuwait and South Yemen) there are neither American nor British banks. Also listed is the central bank of each country.

Bahrain

American Express International
  Banking Corporation
P.O. Box 93
Pearl of Bahrain Bldg.
Government Road
Manama, Bahrain
Telephone: 253600

Bankers Trust Company
P.O. Box 5905
Manama Centre, 1st Floor, West Wing
Government Road
Manama, Bahrain
Telephone: 259841

Bank of America NT and SA
P.O. Box 5280
Pearl of Bahrain Bldg.
Government Road
Manama, Bahrain
Telephone: 50559, 51714, 50768

Chase Manhattan Bank NA
P.O. Box 368
Manama, Bahrain
Telephone: 259831/2

*Source: Middle East Financial Directory 1979, London: Middle East Economic Digest, 1979.

Bahrain
Chemical Bank
P.O. Box 5492
Bank Bldg.
Government Road
Manama, Bahrain
Telephone: 252619, 252630

CitiBank NA
P.O. Box 548
Government Road
Manama, Bahrain
Telephone: 254755

Continental Bank Limited (Chicago)
P.O. Box 5237
BAB Al Bahrain Bldg.
Manama, Bahrain
Telephone: 256228

Manufacturers Hanover Trust Company
P.O. Box 5471
National Bank of Bahrain Tower,
   5th Floor
Government Road
Manama, Bahrain
Telephone: 254375, 254353

Security Pacific National Bank
P.O. Box 5589
Manama Centre
Manama, Bahrain
Telephone: 2599956, 259135, 259137

Texas Commerce Bank
P.O. Box 5777
Kanoo Bldg.
Manama, Bahrain
Telephone: 257575

Central Banking Authority:
Bahrain Monetary Agency
P.O. Box 27
Manama, Bahrain
Telephone: 714023, 712657

Kuwait
No American or British banks.

Central Banking Authority:
Central Bank of Kuwait
P.O. Box 526
Abdullah Al Salim Street
Kuwait
Telephone: 449200

Oman
CitiBank NA
P.O. Box 918
Jaffar House
Muscat, Oman
Telephone: 722662, 722779, 722933

Central Banking Authority:
Central Bank of Oman
P.O. Box 4161
Ruwi, Oman
Telephone: 70222

Qatar
CitiBank NA
P.O. Box 2309
Sheikh Ahmed Bldg.
Rayyan Road
Doha, Qatar
Telephone: 24416–8

Central Banking Authority:
Qatar Monetary Agency
P.O. Box 1234
Doha, Qatar
Telephone: 5987, 25508

Saudi Arabia
CitiBank NA
P.O. Box 490
Taher Bldg.
Sharafia
Jeddah, Saudi Arabia
Telephone: 24155, 24011

Saudi Arabia

Central Banking Authority:
Saudi Arabian Monetary Authority
P.O. Box 2992
Riyadh, Saudi Arabia
Telephone: 201734/7

United Arab Emirates
Abu Dhabi, UAE
Bank of America NT and SA
P.O. Box 3848
Sogex Bldg.
Shaikh Khalifa Street
Abu Dhabi, UAE
Telephone: 26301

Chase Manhattan Bank NA
P.O. Box 3491
Commercial Bank of Dubai Bldg.
Abu Dhabi, UAE
Telephone: 24288, 26489

CitiBank NA
P.O. Box 999
Al Jaber Bldg.
Lulu Street
Abu Dhabi, UAE
Telephone: 41410

The First National Bank of Chicago
P.O. Box 2747
Shaikh Khalifa Bin Zayed Street
Abu Dhabi, UAE
Telephone: 23750

United California Bank
P.O. Box 6643
Ali Bin Ali Bldg.
Abu Dhabi, UAE
Telephone: 21896/7

Dubai, UAE
American Express International
Banking Corporation
P.O. Box 3304
New Shaikh Rashid Bldg.
Al Maktoum Road—Deira
Dubai, UAE

Chemical Bank
P.O. Box 4619
New Shaikh Latifa Ministry Bldg.
Bin Yas Street—Deira
Dubai, UAE
Telephone: 225279, 225270

CitiBank NA
P.O. Box 749
Dubai, UAE
Telephone: 432100

First National Bank in Dallas
P.O. Box 702—Deira
Dubai, UAE
Telephone: 282380

The First National Bank of Chicago
P.O. Box 1655
Al Maktoum Street—Deira
Dubai, UAE
Telephone: 226161–6

Sharjah, UAE
CitiBank NA
P.O. Box 346
H. H. Shaikh Khalid Bldg.
1 Al Arooba Street
Sharjah, UAE
Telephone: 22533, 22583

The First National Bank of Chicago
P.O. Box 1278
Al Arooba Street
Sharjah, UAE
Telephone: 23532, 23982

Ajman, UAE
Grindlays Bank Limited
P.O. Box 452
Ajman, UAE
Telephone: 22007/8

Fujairah, UAE
Grindlays Bank Limited
P.O. Box 92
Fujairah, UAE
Telephone: 22550

Ras Al Khaimah, UAE
CitiBank
P.O. Box 294
Ras Al Khaimah, UAE
Telephone: 29235/6

Umm Al Qaiwain, UAE
Grindlays Bank Limited
P.O. Box 490
Umm Al Qaiwan, UAE
Telephone: 66060

Central Banking Authority:
UAE Currency Board
P.O. Box 854
Abu Dhabi, UAE
Telephone: 43728

North Yemen (Sana)
CitiBank NA
P.O. Box 2133
Zubairi Road
Sana, Yemen
Telephone: 5796

Central Banking Authority:
Central Bank of Yemen
P.O. Box 59
Liberation Square
Sana, Yemen
Telephone: 5215

South Yemen (Aden)
No American or British banks.

National Bank of Yemen
P.O. Box 5
Aidrous Road
Crater, Aden
PDR of Yemen
Telephone: 52252, 52481

Central Banking Authority:
Bank of Yemen
P.O. Box 452
Crater, Aden
PDR of Yemen
Telephone: 51814–7

APPENDIX B

Chiefs of State and Cabinet Members on the Arabian Peninsula*

Shown below is a list of government officials for the eight nations of the Arabian Peninsula. The material is current as of July 1980. (*Note*: Since Westernized adaptations of Arabic words vary, the spellings of names may differ from those in the text.)

Bahrain

Head of State (Amir)	Shaikh Isa bin Salman Al Khalifa
Prime Minister	Shaikh Khalifa bin Salman Al Khalifa
Min. of Commerce and Agriculture	Habib Qassim
Min. of Defense	Shaikh Hamad ibn Isa Al Khalifa
Min. of Development and Industry	Yusuf Ahmad al-Shirawi
Min. of Education	Shaikh 'Abd al-Aziz ibn Muhammad Al Khalifa
Min. of Finance and National Economy	Ibrahim 'Abd al-Karim

Source: National Foreign Assessment Center, "Chiefs of State and Cabinet Members of Foreign Governments," Washington, D.C.: Library of Congress, April 1980.

Min. of Foreign Affairs	Shaikh Mohammad bin Mubarak Al Khalifa
Min. of Health	Ali Muhammad Fakhru
Min. of Housing	Shaikh Khalid ibn Abdallah Al Khalifa
Min. of Information	Tarq 'Abd al-Rahman al-Mu'ayyid
Min. of Interior	Shaikh Muhammad ibn Khalifa ibn Hamid Al Khalifa
Min. of Justice and Islamic Affairs	Shaikh Abdallah ibn Khalid Al Khalifa
Min. of Labor and Social Affairs	Shaikh Isa ibn Muhammad Al Khalifa
Min. of Public Works, Electricity and Water	Majid al-Jishi
Min. of Transportation and Communication	Ibrahim Muhammad Hasan Humaydan
Min. of State for Cabinet Affairs	Jawad Salim al-Urayid
Min. of State for Legal Affairs	Husayn Muhammad al-Baharna

Kuwait

Head of State (Amir)	Shaikh Jabir al-Ahmad Al Sabah
Prime Minister	Shaikh Saad al-Abdullah Al Sabah
Dep. Prime Minister	Shaikh Jabir al-Ali Al Sabah
Dep. Prime Minister	Shaikh Sabah al-Ahmad Al Sabah
Min. for Amiri Diwan Affairs	Shaikh Khalid al-Ahmad al-Jabir Al Sabah
Min. of Commerce and Industry	'Abd al-Wahab al-Nafisi
Min. of Communications	Sulayman Zayd al-Khalid
Min. of Defense	Shaikh Salim al-Sabah al-Salim Al Sabah
Min. of Education	Jasim Khalid al-Marzuq
Min. of Electricity and Water	Khalaf Ahmad al-Khalaf
Min. of Foreign Affairs	Shaikh Sabah al-Ahmad Al Sabah
Min. of Finance	Abdul Rahman Salim al-Ateeqi
Min. of Health	'Abd al-Rahman al-Awadi
Min. of Housing	Hamad Mubarak al-Ayyar
Min. of Information	Shaikh Jabir al-Ali Al Sabah
Min. of Interior	Shaikh Nawaf al-Ahmad al-Jabir Al Sabah
Min. of Justice	Abdallah al-Mufarraj

Min. of Legal and Administrative Affairs	Shaikh Salman al-Duayj Al Sabah
Min. of Oil	Shaikh Ali al-Khalifa Al Sabah
Min. of Planning	Salim Jasim al-Mudhaf
Min. of Public Works	Muhammad al-Adasani
Min. of Religious Trusts and Islamic Affairs	Yusif Jasim al-Hajji
Min. of Social Affairs and Labor	'Abd al-Aziz Mahmud Bu-Shahri
Min. of State for Cabinet Affairs	'Abd al-Aziz Husayn

Oman

Head of State	Sultan Qaboos bin Sa'id
Prime Minister	Sultan Qaboos bin Sa'id
Dep. Prime Minister for Legal Affairs	Fahd ibn Mahmud Al Bu Sa'id
Dep. Prime Minister for Security and Defense Affairs	Fahar ibn Taymur Al Bu Sa'id
Min. of Agriculture and Fisheries	'Abd al-Hafiz Salim Rajab
Min. of Communications	Salim Nasir Al Bu Sa'id
Min. of Defense	Sultan Qaboos bin Sa'id
Min. of Education	Yahya Mahfuz al-Mundhuri
Min. of Electricity and Water	Muhammad Abdallah al-Harithi
Min. of Finance	Sultan Qaboos bin Sa'id
Min. of Health	Mubarak Khaduri
Min. of Industry and Commerce	Muhammad al-Zubayr
Min. of Information and Youth Affairs	'Abd al-Aziz al-Rawwas
Min. of Interior	Badr ibn Sa'ud Al Bu Sa'id
Min. of Justice	Hilal ibn Hamad al-Sammar
Min. of Labor and Social Affairs	Khalfan ibn Nasir Wahaybi
Min. of Land and Municipality Affairs	Ahmad Abdallah al-Ghazali
Min. of National Heritage and Culture	Faysal ibn Ali ibn Faysal Al Bu Sa'id
Min. of Petroleum and Minerals	Sa'id Ahmad al-Shanfari
Min. of Post, Telegraph and Telephone	Karim Ahmad al-Harami
Min. of Public Works	Asim al-Jamali
Min. of Religious Trusts and Islamic Affairs	Walid ibn Zahir al-Hinai

Min. for Royal Diwan Affairs   Hamad ibn Hamud Al Bu Sa'id
Min. of State for Foreign Affairs   Qais Abdul Munim al-Zawawi

Qatar

Head of State (Amir)   Shaikh Khalifa bin Hamad Al
                                      Thani
Prime Minister   Shaikh Khalifa bin Hamad Al
                                      Thani
Min. of Agriculture and Industry   Shaikh Faysal bin Thani Al Thani
Min. of Commerce and Economy   Shaikh Nasir bin Khalid Al Thani
Min. of Defense   Shaikh Hamad bin Khalifa Al
                                      Thani
Min. of Education   Shaikh Muhammad bin Habad Al
                                      Thani
Min. of Electricity and Water   Shaikh Jasim bin Muhammad Al
  Resources   Thani
Min. of Finance and Petroleum   Shaikh 'Abd al-Aziz bin Khalifa Al
                                      Thani
Min. of Foreign Affairs   Shaikh Suhaim bin Hamad Al
                                      Thani
Min. of Information   Isa Ghanim al-Kawari
Min. of Interior   Shaikh Khalid bin Hamad Al
                                      Thani

Min. of Justice
Min. of Labor and Social Affairs   Ali bin Ahmad al-Ansari
Min. of Municipal Affairs   Shaikh Muhammad bin Jabr Al
                                      Thani
Min. of Public Health   Khalid Muhammad al-Mani
Min. of Public Works   Khalid bin Abdallah al-Atiya
Min. of Transportation and
  Communications   Abdallah bin Nasir al-Suwaydi
Min. of State for Foreign Affairs   Shaikh Ahmad bin Saif Al Thani

Saudi Arabia

Head of State   King Khalid ibn 'Abd al-Aziz Al
                                      Sa'ud
Prime Minister   King Khalid ibn 'Abd al-Aziz Sa'ud
Dep. Prime Minister   Crown Prince Fahd bin 'Abd
                                      al-Aziz Al Sa'ud

2nd Dep. Prime Minister	Prince Abdallah bin 'Abd al-Aziz Al Sa'ud
Min. of Agriculture and Water	'Abd al-Rahman ibn 'Abd al-Aziz Hasan al-Shaykh
Min. of Commerce	Soliman Abdulaziz Solaim
Min. of Communications	Husayn Ibrahim al-Mansur
Min. of Defense and Aviation	Prince Sultan ibn 'Abd al-Aziz Al Sa'ud
Min. of Education	'Abd al-Aziz Abdallah al-Khuwaytir
Min. of Finance and National Economy	Muhammad Ali Aba al-Khayl
Min. of Foreign Affairs	Prince Sa'ud Al Faysal
Min. of Health	Husayn 'Abd al-Razaq al-Jaza'iri
Min. of Higher Education	Hasan ibn Abdallah al-Shaykh
Min. of Industry and Electricity	Ghazi al-Gosaibi
Min. of Information	Muhammad Abduh Yamani
Min. of Interior	Prince Nayif ibn 'Abd al-Aziz Al Sa'ud
Min. of Justice	Ibrahim ibn Muhammad ibn Ibrahim al-Shaykh
Min. of Labor and Social Affairs	Ibrahim ibn Abdallah al-Anqari
Min. of Municipal and Rural Affairs	Prince Majid ibn 'Abd al-Aziz Al Sa'ud
Min. of Petroleum and Mineral Resources	Ahamad Zaki Yamani
Min. of Pilgrimage Affairs and Religious Trusts	'Abd al-Wahab 'Abd al-Wasi
Min. of Planning	Hisham Muhyi al-Din Naser
Min. of Post, Telephone and Telegraph	Alawi Darwish Kayyal
Min. of Public Works and Housing	Prince Majid ibn 'Abd al-Aziz Al Sa'ud
Min. of State	Muhammad Ibrahim Mas'ud
Min. of State	Muhammad 'Abd al-Latif al-Mulhim
Min. of State	'Abd al-Aziz ibn Zayd al-Qurayshi

United Arab Emirates

President	Shaikh Zayid bin Sultan Al Nahayyan (Ruler of Abu Dhabi)
Vice President	Shaikh Rashid ibn Sa'id Al Maktum (Ruler of Dubai)
Prime Minister	Shaikh Rashid ibn Sa'id Al Maktum
Dep. Prime Minister	Shaikh Maktum ibn Rashid Al Maktum
Dep. Prime Minister	Shaikh Hamdan ibn Muhammad Al Nahayyan
Min. of Agriculture and Fisheries	Sa'id al-Raqbani
Min. of Communications	Muhammad Sa'id al-Mulla
Min. of Defense	Shaikh Muhammad ibn Rashid ibn Sa'id Al Maktum
Min. of Economy and Trade	Shaikh Sultan ibn Ahmad Al Mu'alla
Min. of Education and Youth	Sa'id Salman
Min. of Electricity and Water	Humayd Nasir al-'Uways
Min. of Finance and Industry	Shaikh Hamdan ibn Rashid ibn Sa'id Al Maktum
Min. of Foreign Affairs	Ahmad Khalifa al-Suwaidi
Min. of Health	Hamad 'Abd al-Rahman al-Madia
Min. of Information and Culture	Shaikh Ahmad ibn Hamid Al Nahayyan
Min. of Interior	Shaikh Mubarak ibn Muhammad Al Nahayyan
Min. of Justice, Islamic Affairs and Religious Trusts	Muhammad 'Abd al-Rahman al-Bakr
Min. of Labor and Social Affairs	Sayf Ali al-Jarwan
Min. of Petroleum and Mineral Resources	Mani ibn Sa'id al-Utayba
Min. of Planning	Sa'id Ahamd al-Ghubash
Min. of Public Works and Housing	Muhammad Khalifa al-Kindi
Min. of State	Shaikh Ahmad ibn Sultan Al Qasimi
Min. of State for Cabinet Affairs	Sa'id al-Ghayth
Min. of State for Foreign Affairs	Rashid Abdallah Ali al-Nu'aymi
Min. of State for Supreme Council Affairs	Shaikh 'Abd al-Aziz ibn Hamid Al Qasimi

Yemen Arab Republic

President	Ali Abdullah Saleh
Prime Minister	'Abd al-Aziz 'Abd al-Ghani
Min. of Development	Ali Lutfi al-Thawr
Min. of Economy	Muhammad Hizan Shuhati
Min. of Education	Muhammad al-Khadim al-Wajih
Min. of Finance	Ahmad 'Abd al-Rahman Samawi
Min. of Foreign Affairs	Hasan Makki
Min. of Health	Muhammad Ahmad al-Ashabi
Min. of Information and Culture	Yahya Husayn al-Arashi
Min. of Interior	Muhammad Hamud Khamis
Min. of Justice	Isma'il Ahmad Wazir
Min. of Labor, Social Affairs and Youth	Ahamd Salih Ruayni
Min. of Municipalities	Ahmad al-Mihanni
Min. of Public Works	Abdallah al-Kurshumi
Min. of Religious Trusts and Guidance	Ali Sam'an
Min. of Supply and Trade	Salih al-Jamali
Min. of State	Husayn al-Hubayshi
Min. of State for Information Affairs	Lutfi al-Kilabi
Min. of State for Petroleum and Mineral Affairs	Ahamd Qaid Barakat

People's Democratic Republic of Yemen

Chmn., Presidium, Supreme People's Council	Ali Nasir Muhammad al-Hasani
Sec., Presidium, Supreme People's Council	Fadi Muhsin Abdallah
Mbr., Presidium, Supreme People's Council	Faris Salim Ahmad
Mbr., Presidium, Supreme People's Council	Riyad al-Akbari
Mbr., Presidium, Supreme People's Council	Sultan Muhammad al-Dawsh
Mbr., Presidium, Supreme People's Council	Abdallah Ahmad al-Ghanim

Mbr., Presidium, Supreme People's
  Council   Aidah Ali Sa'id

Mbr., Presidium, Supreme People's
  Council   Mahmud Sa'id al-Madhi

Mbr., Presidium, Supreme People's
  Council   Ali Ahmad Nasir Salami

Mbr., Presidium, Supreme People's
  Council   Sa'id Salih Salim
Chmn., Council of Ministers   Ali Nasir Muhammad al-Hasani
Min. of Agriculture and Agrarian
  Reform   Fadl Muhsin Abdallah
Min. of Building   Haider Abu Bakr
Min. of Communications   Mahmud Abdallah Rashid
                                           'Ushaysh
Min. of Culture and Tourism   Mahmud Najashi
Min. of Defense   'Ali Ahmad Nasir (Antar) al-Bishi
Min. of Education   Sa'id 'Abd al-Khir al-Nuban
Min. of Finance   Mahmud Sa'id al-Madhi
Min. of Fish Resources   Anis Hassan
Min. of Foreign Affairs   Salim Salih Muhammad
Min. of Health   Abdallah Ahmad Bukayr
Min. of Industry   'Abd al-Ghani 'Abd al-Qadir
Min. of Installations   Haydar Abu Bakr al-Attas
Min. of Interior   Ali Shay'i Hadi
Min. of Justice and Religious
  Trusts   Khalid Fadl Mansur
Min. of Labor and Civil Service   Nasir Nasir Ali
Min. of Planning   Faraj Ghanim
Min. of Trade and Supply   Ahamd 'Ubayd al-Fadli
Min. of State for Council of
  Ministers   Ali Asad Muthana

APPENDIX C

Airlines Serving the Arabian Peninsula*

A list of flights into the target countries is shown below. This is but a brief list to provide some idea of the availability of flights.

Country	Airline	Approx. Frequency	To/From
Bahrain–Muharraq	Gulf Air British Air Qantas Singapore Air	Daily	London
Kuwait–Kuwait City	Kuwait Airlines British Air	Daily	London
Oman–Muscat	Gulf Air British Air	Daily	London
Qatar–Doha	Gulf Air British Air	Daily	London

*Source: Official Airlines Guide, World Wide Edition, April 1980.

Country	Airline	Approx. Frequency	To/From
UAE–Abu Dhabi	Gulf Air British Air Singapore Air Japan Air	Daily	London
UAE–Dubai	Gulf Air British Air Pakistan Int'l Singapore Air	Daily	London
Saudi Arabia–Dhahran	Saudia Air British Air	Daily	London
	Saudia Air Pan American	Daily (Nonstop)	New York
Saudi Arabia–Jeddah	Saudia Air British Air	Daily	London
Saudi Arabia–Riyadh	Saudia Air	Daily	London
North Yemen–Sana	Air France	Varies	Cairo
	Saudia Air Yemen Air Egypt Air Kuwait Air	Daily	Jeddah
South Yemen–Aden	Saudia Air Middle East Air	Varies	Jeddah
	Kuwait Air	Varies	Kuwait

APPENDIX D

Selected Bibliography

General Information on the Middle East

1. American University, *Area Handbook for the Peripheral States of the Arabian Peninsula*. Washington, D.C.: Government Printing Office, 1971.
2. _____, *Area Handbook for the Yemens*. Washington, D.C.: Government Printing Office, 1977.
3. _____, *Area Handbook for the Persian Gulf States*. Washington, D.C.: Government Printing Office, 1977.
4. _____, *Area Handbook for Saudi Arabia*. Washington, D.C.: Government Printing Office, 1977.
5. *Arabic for Travelers*. Lausanne, Switz.: Berlitz, 1975.
6. Caldwell, Wallace E., *The Ancient World*. New York: Holt, Rinehart, and Winston, 1965.
7. Coon, Carlton S., *Caravan: The Story of the Middle East*. New York: Henry Holt, 1951.
8. Curtis, Jerry L., *Bahrain: Language, Customs, and People*. England: Tien Wah Press Ltd., n.d.
9. Hitti, Phillip K., *The Arabs—A Short History*. Chicago: Henry Regnery Co., 1964.
10. Isenberg, Irwin, *The Arab World*. New York: H. W. Wilson Co., 1976.

11. *The Middle East and North Africa* 1979–80. London: Europa Publications, 1979.
12. Travintal, *Arab Countries—Handbook for Businessman & Traveler*. Athens: Athens Publishing Center, 1976.
13. *United Arab Emirates: A Travel Handbook*. Greece: Travel International, n.d.
14. U.S. Central Intelligence Agency, *Issues in the Middle East*. Washington, D.C.: Government Printing Office, 1973.
15. U.S. Department of Defense, *A Pocket Guide to the Middle East*. Washington, D.C.: Government Printing Office, n.d.
16. U.S. Department of State, *Background Notes: Kuwait*. Washington, D.C.: Government Printing Office, 1977.
17. _____, *Background Notes: Oman*. Washington, D.C.: Government Printing Office, 1978.
18. _____, *Background Notes: Qatar*. Washington, D.C.: Government Printing Office, 1979.
19. _____, *Background Notes: United Arab Emirates*. Washington, D.C.: Government Printing Office, 1977.
20. _____, *Background Notes: Saudi Arabia*. Washington D.C.: Government Printing Office, 1979.
21. _____, *Background Notes: Bahrain*. Washington, D.C.: Government Printing Office, 1977.
22. _____, *Background Notes: (North) Yemen*. Washington, D.C.: Government Printing Office, 1977.
23. _____, *Background Notes: (South) Yemen*. Washington, D.C.: Government Printing Office, 1977.
24. Wazaifi, Rashid, *The Arabian Year Book—1978*. London: Kelly's Directories Ltd., 1978.

Cultural, Political, and Social Information on the Middle East

1. Alireza, Marianne, *At the Drop of a Veil*. Boston: Houghton Mifflin Co., 1971.
2. Berger, Morroe, *The Arab World Today*. New York: Anchor Books, 1962.
3. Bibby, Geoffrey, *Looking for Dilmun*. London: Collins, 1970.
4. Blandford, Linda, *Oil Sheikhs*. London: W. H. Allen & Co., 1976.
5. Dawood, N. J., trans., *The Koran*. Middlesex, Eng.: Penguin Books, 1956.

6. Gibb, H. A. R., *Mohammedanism*. New York: Oxford University Press, 1962.
7. Guillaume, Alfred, *Islam*. Middlesex, Eng.: Penguin Books, 1954.
8. Harari, Maurice, *Government and Politics of the Middle East*. Englewood Cliffs, N. J.: Prentice-Hall, 1962.
9. Howarth, David, *The Desert King: A Life of Ibn Saud*. London: Collins, 1964.
10. Laffin, John, *The Arab Mind—A Need for Understanding*. New York: Taplinger Publishing Company, 1975.
11. Patai, Raphael, *The Arab Mind*. New York: Charles Scribner's Sons, 1976.
12. Schvow, Frithjof, *Understanding Islam*. Baltimore: Penguin Books, 1961.
13. Sharabi, Hisham B., *Nationalism and Revolution in the Arab World*. Princeton, N. J.: D. Van Nostrand Co., 1966.
14. _____, *Government and Politics of the Middle East in the Twentieth Century*. Princeton, N. J.: D. Van Nostrand Co., 1962.
15. Thesiger, Wilfred, *Arabian Sands*. Continent Books Ltd., n.d.
16. Thompson, J. H., and R. D. Reischaver, *Modernization in the Arab World*. Princeton, N. J.: D. Van Nostrand Co., 1966.

Business and Economics in the Middle East

1. Africano, Lillian, *The Businessman's Guide to the Middle East*. New York: Harper & Row, 1977.
2. Ahmed, Samir, *Saudi Arabia*. New York: Chase World Information, 1976.
3. *The Arab Business Year Book*. London: Graham & Trotman Ltd., 1980.
4. *Arab Markets—1979–80*. New York: Inter-Crescent Publishing, 1980.
5. Beck, Louis, and Nikki Keddie, *Women in the Muslim World*. Cambridge, Mass.: Harvard University Press, 1978.
6. *Business Guide to Saudi Arabia*. Seven Arabian Markets Ltd. (no city or date).
7. *Businessman's Guide to the Arab World and Iran—1978*. Boston: Harvard Square, 1977.
8. *Doing Business in Kuwait*, New York: Price Waterhouse, 1975.
9. *Doing Business in Oman*, New York: Price Waterhouse, 1976.
10. *Doing Business in Saudi Arabia*, New York: Price Waterhouse, 1975.

11. *Doing Business in the United Arab Emirates,* New York: Price Water-house, 1976.
12. Field, Michael, *A Hundred Million Dollars a Day.* London: Sidgwick & Jackson Ltd., 1975.
13. Haiek, Joseph R., *Mideast Business Guide.* Los Angeles: Mideast Business Exchange, 1977.
14. Hunter, MacLean, *Guide to the Middle East.* London: by the author, 1979.
15. *Investment Guide to the Arabian Gulf.* New York: First National City Bank, n.d.
16. Izzard, Molly, and John Murray, *The Gulf: Arabia's Western Approaches.* London: by the authors, 1979.
17. Karam, Nicola H., *Business Laws of Saudi Arabia.* London: Graham & Trotman Ltd., 1977.
18. Khouja, M. W., and P. G. Sadler, *The Economy of Kuwait.* London: MacMillan Press, 1979.
19. London Chamber of Commerce, *Trade Contacts in the Arab World.* London: Kogan Page, n.d.
20. *Middle East Annual Review—1980.* London: The Middle East Review Co. Ltd., 1979.
21. Middle East Economic Digest, *Middle East Financial Directory 1979,* London: Bourne, 1979.
22. *Middle East Year Book—1980,* London: IC Magazines Ltd., 1980.
23. *People's Democratic Republic of Yemen: A Review of Economic and Social Development.* Washington, D.C.: World Bank, 1979.
24. *A Practical Guide to Living and Travel in the Arab World.* New York: Inter-Crescent Publishing, 1978.
25. Russell, Brian, *Business Law in the Middle East.* London: Oyez Publishing, 1975.
26. Sadik, Muhammad, and William P. Snavely, *Bahrain, Qatar, and the United Arab Emirates: Colonial Past, Present Problems, and Future Prospects.* London: D. C. Heath, 1972.
27. Sampson, Anthony, *The Seven Sisters.* London: Hodder and Stoughton, 1975.
28. *A Selected Directory of Business Contracts in the Arab World.* New York: Inter-Crescent Publishing, 1978.
29. Shilling, Nancy A., *Doing Business in Saudi Arabia and the Gulf States.* New York: Inter-Crescent Publishing, 1975.
30. U.S. Department of Commerce, *A Business Guide to the Near East and North Africa.* Washington, D.C.: Government Printing Office, 1978.

31. _____, *An Introduction to Contract Procedures in the Near East and North Africa*. Washington, D.C.: Government Printing Office, 1979.

32. _____, *Foreign Economic Trends: Kuwait, 79-107*. Washington, D.C.: Government Printing Office, 1979.

33. _____ *Foreign Economic Trends: Oman, 79-044*. Washington, D.C.: Government Printing Office, 1979.

34. _____, *Foreign Economic Trends: Qatar, 79-106*. Washington, D.C.: Government Printing Office, 1979.

35. _____, *Foreign Economic Trends: United Arab Emirates, 79-085*. Washington, D.C.: Government Printing Office, 1979.

36. _____, *Overseas Business Report: Marketing in Kuwait, OBR 79-81*. Washington, D.C.: Government Printing Office, 1979.

37. _____, *Overseas Business Report: Marketing in the United Arab Emirates, OBR 77–64*, Washington, D.C.: Government Printing Office, 1977.

38. _____, *Overseas Business Report: World Trade Outlook for Near East and North Africa, OBR 79-09*. Washington, D.C.: Government Printing Office, 1979.

39. _____, *Overseas Business Report: Near East / North Africa Business Costs, OBR 79-19*. Washington, D.C.: Government Printing Office, 1979.

40. Wilson, Rodney, *Trade and Investment in the Middle East*. London: MacMillan Press, 1977.

41. *Working for Northrop in Saudi Arabia*, Los Angeles: Northrop Corporation, n.d.

42. *Yemen Arab Republic: Development of a Traditional Economy*. Washington, D.C.: World Bank, 1979.